D1383172

Computing with the Raspberry Pi
Command Line and GUI Linux

Brian Schell

Apress®

Computing with the Raspberry Pi: Command Line and GUI Linux

Brian Schell
Flint, MA, USA

ISBN-13 (pbk): 978-1-4842-5292-5   ISBN-13 (electronic): 978-1-4842-5293-2
https://doi.org/10.1007/978-1-4842-5293-2

Managing Director, Apress Media LLC: Welmoed Spahr
Acquisitions Editor: Aaron Black
Development Editor: James Markham
Coordinating Editor: Jessica Vakili

Cover designed by eStudioCalamar

Cover image designed by Freepik (www.freepik.com)

Distributed to the book trade worldwide by Springer Science+Business Media New York, 233 Spring Street, 6th Floor, New York, NY 10013. Phone 1-800-SPRINGER, fax (201) 348-4505, e-mail orders-ny@springer-sbm.com, or visit www.springeronline.com. Apress Media, LLC is a California LLC and the sole member (owner) is Springer Science + Business Media Finance Inc (SSBM Finance Inc). SSBM Finance Inc is a **Delaware** corporation.

For information on translations, please e-mail rights@apress.com, or visit http://www.apress.com/rights-permissions.

Apress titles may be purchased in bulk for academic, corporate, or promotional use. eBook versions and licenses are also available for most titles. For more information, reference our Print and eBook Bulk Sales web page at http://www.apress.com/bulk-sales.

Any source code or other supplementary material referenced by the author in this book is available to readers on GitHub via the book's product page, located at www.apress.com/978-1-4842-5292-5. For more detailed information, please visit http://www.apress.com/source-code.

Printed on acid-free paper

Remembering my first computer: a Sinclair ZX81.

The Raspberry Pi costs one-fifth as much and is a million times more powerful.

Table of Contents

TABLE OF CONTENTS

About the Author

Brian Schell lives in Flint, Michigan, and is primarily a technology writer. He does professional editing and audiobook narration in his spare time as well. He's spent time in Japan, taught English both abroad and in the United States, and is an avid amateur radio operator and all-around technology addict.

With an educational background in religion studies and English composition, as well as a long history of entrepreneurship and business management, he brings an unusual perspective to most topics.

Introduction

Why Do This?

More and more, minimalism is becoming the way of life for a lot of people. Minimalism doesn't mean poverty; it means efficiently doing more with less. Less clutter, less junk, less debt, less stress, and generally less on our minds. Who wouldn't want that? There are even very successful shows on TV about decluttering your life and making your household simpler by eliminating the things that don't make you happy. We can all benefit by making a lower ecological footprint, incurring less debt, and not by chasing "the Joneses."

This book isn't about cleaning up your house. It's about cleaning up your technology, or at least in learning how to do all the same stuff you already do in as minimal a way as possible. If you're used to working from a $2500 MacBook Pro, or if you have three iPads in your living room, and you're just waiting for the next new phone upgrade, then I may be talking to you. We all love expensive new high-tech toys, but it's a lot of fun going the other direction as well. What's the least equipment you need to get by?

The first thing that comes to mind is by using older equipment. You can buy used computers on dozens of web sites, and that's always an option. Still, they're old equipment, they're used, and who knows how reliable they are after the previous owner did...whatever with them? I always prefer new equipment, but I just don't want to spend a lot of money. I like configuring that equipment to my specifications and making it all work my way.

What kind of computer can we get that's new, but really inexpensive? Well, junk computers usually. You can buy a cheap, new Windows laptop for $200, but it will come preloaded with a ton of bloatware, run slowly, and make the user experience worse than nothing. Chromebooks are an awesome concept, and they're very powerful in themselves with little cost, but there's almost no customization possible, and they are also closely intertwined with cloud computing, which has its own drawbacks. These obvious solutions aren't really solutions at all, they just create new problems. We're going to have to look off the mainstream path for what we want.

I suggest the Raspberry Pi (RPi). This little computer has a quad-core processor, more USB ports than any MacBook made today, and it runs many different varieties of Linux, the most stable free operating system in use today. And best of all, it's really, really inexpensive for new hardware.

Why the Raspberry Pi over one of the many newer all-in-one single-board computers that have sprung up since the Raspberry first hit the market? Why not an Arduino, BeagleBone, Odroid, Tinker Board, RockPro, or even Le Potato? Yes, that last one is a real product. Those are all powerful little computers that have their purpose. The Arduino is great for electronics applications that need a microcontroller. The Tinker Board is good for, well, tinkering. The Raspberry Pi, however, can do all these things in a very general-purpose way; what we are looking for in this book is a small device that can serve as a general-purpose computer, and in my opinion, the Pi is the best all-around device for this. There's a reason so many of these competitors look just like a souped-up Raspberry Pi: because they are. They took the best and bumped it up a little. By sticking with the established Pi architecture, you get the benefit of the most tested and evolved selection of software. Many of those other devices require you to compile the operating system and jump through hoops just to get a working system; the millions of Pi hobbyists have done all that for us already. Many of the apps we will look at here, especially on the desktop side, are simply not available for many of these other devices.

Although all the advertising for Raspberry Pi points out that "It's only $35," that's not strictly true, as this cost is just for the main motherboard. You'll also need a power supply, memory card, a case of some kind, and a few cables. You can pick up the parts individually quite easily, or there are kits that have everything you need for around the same price. Assuming you can scrounge up your own keyboard, mouse, and monitor, you'll still only be out of pocket fifty to sixty dollars USD for the other parts.

Most books on the Raspberry Pi focus on programming, hardware tinkering, and electronics interfacing. Not this book. We won't deal with the GPIO port at all, nor will we do any coding of any kind here. In this book, we'll look at setting up a Raspberry Pi with the intention of using it as a real computer. We'll install real desktop software and do real work on it. Then we'll look under the hood and learn all the command-line tools that will really make things speed along and do things you wouldn't dream you could do with such a small device. Are there limits to what we can do with this little computer? Yes, and that's where the challenge comes in. It'll be fun, it'll be inexpensive, and it'll be minimalist computing in the extreme!

Let's get started! In the first chapter, we'll look at the hardware aspect of this project. What will you need to buy? What have you already got? And how do we make it all work?

CHAPTER 1

Setting Up the Raspberry Pi As a Computer

In this chapter, we'll look at the hardware aspect of our project. We'll go over all the options for hardware and parts; then we'll assemble everything. The biggest part of the project is installing the basic operating system, and going through the initial setup phase of Raspbian, the Raspberry Pi operating system.

If you've ever assembled a desktop computer, this is essentially the same process, but everything is just a little different on the Pi. If you've never "built" a computer before, then you're in for a fun chapter; once you've got all the parts, the rest is just a matter of following the instructions.

It's obvious why you need the hardware; you wouldn't have a computer without the physical parts. But why do we need to install an operating system? You don't usually need to do that with a Mac or Windows computer, so why is this necessary for the Pi? The simplest reasons are *freedom* and *choices*.

If you have a Mac, you're going to run MacOS (formerly OSX). If you have a consumer-style PC, it's going to come with Windows 10. You don't need to install anything; just plug them in and they'll work, but you don't

© Brian Schell 2019
B. Schell, *Computing with the Raspberry Pi*, https://doi.org/10.1007/978-1-4842-5293-2_1

get to choose. You generally don't run Windows on a Mac or MacOS on a PC. There's no choice.

The Raspberry Pi, on the other hand, runs the Linux operating system rather than MacOS or Windows. Linux is a free operating system that was created and is maintained by volunteers working for free. These millions of volunteers are constantly improving and debugging and working tirelessly so that there *are* alternatives to MacOS and Windows.

Like with any large group, when you have that many developers, it's hard to get everyone to agree on what's best, so there are numerous different types of Linux. These different flavors are called *distributions*. Each one is essentially the same at the core, and that's what makes them Linux; but there are many aspects of the operating system that are optional, like what the desktop looks like, how the setup screens work, what apps are included, which web browser is the default, and things like that. There are about a dozen different distributions of Linux that work on the Raspberry Pi, and we'll only be focusing heavily on one of them; but at any time, it's easy to set up and use a different version, and surprisingly enough, it's a lot of fun—you may want to try several and see which one works the most like what you want in a computer.

Hardware Requirements and Notes on Getting Started

I said we'd be going minimal here, and I wasn't kidding. There aren't any tricks or hidden costs here. There are no subscription services to pay every month, and no extra hardware is needed; but most of the usual PC hardware accessories, like hard drives, flash drives, fancy mice, keyboards, and Bluetooth devices, can be optionally used, so you don't have to limit yourself to the basics.

Here's a quick "shopping list" of things you probably don't have lying around already. All prices are in US dollars:

- Raspberry Pi model 4 system board ($35–$55).

- 5.1V/3.0A DC output power supply with micro-USB plug (around $8).

- Micro SD card with 8GB capacity or more (around $6).

- Some kind of enclosure or case made for the model 4 system.

- CanaKit (and other sources) offers a complete starter kit with case, power supply, heat sinks, SD card, and Raspberry Pi main board for $79.95 at the time of this writing.

  Alternatively,

- Raspberry Pi model 3B+ system board (around $35)

- 3.5A power supply with micro-USB plug (around $7)

- Micro SD card with 8GB capacity or more (around $6)

- Some kind of enclosure or case made for the 3B+ system ($6 and up)

The following are additional things to consider:

- **Motherboard:** For the system board, you *can* use older Raspberry Pi models instead of the 4 or 3B+, but I wouldn't recommend it. The Pi model 2s were quite a bit slower and also required a dongle for Wi-Fi and Bluetooth. Wi-Fi and Bluetooth are built-in with the model 3 Pi. Also, the 3B+ is faster and has better networking speed than the original 3B. The Raspberry Pi Zero is a current device, but has significantly less

3

processor power, and we need that power with many desktop applications. It's only logical that for maximum power, we want the newest and most powerful Pi, which is the model 4 (as of this writing). You can use the Pi Zero or the older versions if you want, but same apps may have difficulties that are hard to predict. Everything mentioned in this book has been thoroughly tested with the model 3B+ and 4.

- **Model 3B+ Power Supply:** Depending on your phone, the charger you use for it *might* work fine here. Check the amperage and that it uses a micro-USB plug. Most Android phones have this plug, but iPhones don't. The power requirements for the Raspberry Pi model 3 are 5V and 2.5A. The Pi model 2 and some older models can use 2A power supplies, but the models 3 and 3+ are stricter in requiring a steady 2.5A. If in doubt, buy an approved power supply. Various models are available online ranging from $7 to $10.

- **Model 4 Power Supply:** The newer model 4 RPi boards take their power from a USB-C connector, not the micro-USB of all the previous models. They also have a generally higher power consumption than any previous system. You'll need a 15.3W USB-C power supply for the model 4. Again, a phone charger might work, but to be safe get the approved power supply.

- **Micro SD Card:** You can use almost any micro SD card if you have one lying around, but the ones marked "class 10" are the fastest. This is essentially our boot-up hard drive, so any speed bump we can get in this area is good. The "official" maximum size for the card is 32GB.

Although there are reports of some larger sizes that work, there are no guarantees, and some larger cards definitely *do not work*. My recommendation is to get an 8–16GB class 10 card to start, depending on what kind of a deal you can get. Later on, we'll look at setting up the Pi to boot from an actual external hard drive, and this will be a better, safer solution for storing larger quantities of data. A new 16GB card is available for less than $6 as I write this, so if you have a slow card already, I'd recommend splurging on a new one.

- **Case:** I've seen plenty of people use the Pi with the exposed board lying on the tabletop. It works, but I wouldn't recommend it. Get a case that you like. If you are going to be using this system for any length of time, you'll want to keep dust and dirt off of the board, and you'll need to handle the computer to plug in the power supply and various USB cables. A nice case just protects everything and makes it all look good. There are cheap plastic cases available for as low as $6 and some fancy hand-carved wooden ones for upward of $50. They all work essentially the same, so cheap is fine. There are some high-end cases that include fans, but this is almost certainly not necessary for the kinds of software we'll be running. I'd recommend getting the cheapest case you can find, but don't be afraid to splurge later. If you're handy with wood, or if you have a 3D printer, you can even make your own! Also, keep in mind that the model 4 has a completely different port layout than any older model, so a case made for a model 3 *will not work* for a model 4.

Here are some other things you'll need that you may already have:

- Keyboard

- Mouse

- Monitor

- HDMI cable for connecting the Pi to your monitor

With the introduction of the Raspberry Pi model 4 in June of 2019, the Raspberry Pi Foundation also introduced an official keyboard and mouse for the Pi. These are attractively color-coordinated to match the official Pi case, and the keyboard has a "raspberry button" on it in the usual "system key location," but otherwise, they are not required. You can use any USB mouse or keyboard, and these can be either wired with USB or they can use Bluetooth for their connections. Other than that, you can use the same keyboard and mouse you had for your old computer.

Any standard monitor will work, but you'll need a cable with a micro-HDMI plug to connect with your model 4 Pi or a full-size HDMI port to plug into any of the previous models. If you are using the Raspberry Pi model 4, you also have the option of using *two* monitors at once if you choose. Obviously, you would need two monitors and two *micro-HDMI* cables to take advantage of the dual-monitor capability.

Creating the Initial Boot Media

Initially, we'll need to download the operating system software and install it on the SD card. This will require a separate computer running Windows, Mac, or Linux. If you really can't make that work, there are many places that will sell you a SD card with the software already installed; a simple Google search will find a source in your country.

You will need a micro SD card and adaptor to fit the card into whatever slot your computer has.

There are many distributions, or "brands," of Linux that are easily available. Two of the most popular are Raspbian and Ubuntu MATE. Both of these focus on different things: Raspbian is the "official" operating system of the Raspberry Pi, and Ubuntu MATE is a much heavier, desktop-oriented operating system. Raspbian is faster and more efficient, while MATE is easier to use and includes more built-in software, but it is also slower.

The current version of Ubuntu MATE as of this writing is 18.04, which was released in April of 2018. That sounds "old," but Ubuntu has an update system in place where they offer something called LTS, or "Long-Term Support," edition of their operating system. They guarantee support for an LTS version for up to 4 years. The downside of this is that they only release a new version every 2 years. So there won't be new LTS edition until April of 2020. Ubuntu does offer upgrades to its regular operating system every 6 months, but they don't do it for the Raspberry Pi version. So we're all stuck in 2018 for a while.

Ubuntu MATE can be found at `https://ubuntu-mate.org/download/`.

Raspbian, on the other hand, is released on an irregular schedule whenever enough changes accumulate. The latest version as of this writing is called "Buster" (June of 2019). If you want the cutting edge, most "official" version of the Raspberry Pi operating system, this is the one to use.

I'll mostly be focusing on Raspbian in this book, but I will occasionally point out something that can be done differently in MATE. One of the great things about the Raspberry Pi is that for the cost of a second SD card, you can switch back and forth very quickly. Why not try both?

Raspbian can be found at `www.raspberrypi.org/downloads/raspbian/`.

The next piece of software that we'll need is a special utility to copy the operating system to the SD card and make it bootable. The easiest application I've found to do this is **balenaEtcher**, usually just referred to as Etcher. There is a version available for Windows, Mac, and Linux; so wherever you're coming from, they make a version for you.

balenaEtcher can be found at `www.balena.io/etcher/`.

> **Note**   It is also possible to create an SD card image from the
> command line from MacOS or Linux, but it is complex and not at
> all possible from Windows. For the sake of maximum compatibility
> and simplicity, I'm going to stick with Etcher here. If you need to do
> it from the command line, the official documentation can be found
> here: `www.raspberrypi.org/documentation/installation/`
> `installing-images/README.md`.

The process of creating a bootable SD card is simple once you have
the preceding ingredients. Download one of the operating system files,
either Ubuntu MATE or Raspbian. Whichever you choose, you'll end up
downloading one large file.

Once that's done, launch Etcher, and it should look like Figure 1-1.

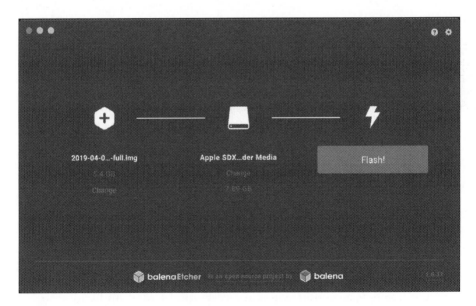

Figure 1-1. *balenaEtcher with source file and destination drive*
selected

There are three buttons/icons. Click the one on the left, and it will allow you to choose a disk image. This is either the Raspbian or Ubuntu MATE file you just finished downloading.

Insert an SD card into the computer. You may need to use an adaptor, dongle, or hub to make it fit. Once the computer recognizes the card, click the middle icon to select the card. Make absolutely sure not to select the wrong disk, as you can delete your computer's hard drive if you aren't careful!

When you're done selecting the operating system file and the target drive, then click the third icon, "Flash!" This will begin the process of formatting the SD card and copying the operating system onto it. This process may take 5–10 minutes depending on various factors, as in Figure 1-2.

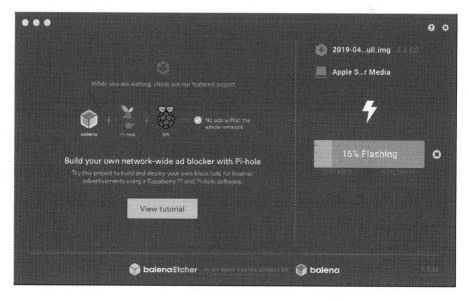

Figure 1-2. *Etcher partway through flashing*

Once the process has completed, Etcher will tell you that it has flashed the card successfully, or it will give you an error message. If there's an error, follow Etcher's suggestions and figure out why. Assuming it worked, you can eject the card and proceed to assembling your Pi.

Assembling the Computer

The following lists outline the required and optional assembly parts:

- **Required Parts**

  - Raspberry Pi motherboard

  - Power supply

  - Micro SD card with an operating system installed on it (from the previous section)

  - Mouse

  - Keyboard

  - Monitor

  - Monitor cable

- **Optional Parts**

  - Case for motherboard

  - Audio listening device (headphones, earbuds, or speakers or just plug it into your monitor's input) with either 3.5mm jack or Bluetooth capability

  - Ethernet cable to plug into your router if you aren't using Wi-Fi

Assembly Instructions

Assuming you have purchased or scrounged all the necessary pieces, assembling the Raspberry Pi into a desktop computer is very easy, as it should be obvious where all the cables go.

1. Insert your Raspberry Pi motherboard into your chosen case and assemble it using whatever instructions come with the case. If your case came with some form of heat sink, be careful not to get fingerprints on either the top of the processor or the bottom of the heat sink.

2. Slide the micro SD card into the slot on the underside of the Raspberry Pi.

3. Plug in the HDMI cable into the monitor and the RPi.

4. Plug in the audio cable into speakers, headphones, or your monitor.

5. Plug in the mouse and keyboard into any of the four USB ports. If you have other USB items, I would recommend sticking with just the mouse and keyboard for now; add other peripherals after those are working. It's *probably* OK to use a Bluetooth mouse or keyboard at this stage, as these *should* be detected on startup. In the rare chance that they aren't, a wired keyboard or mouse may be needed to get the settings configured.

6. Plug in the Ethernet cable if you aren't going to use Wi-Fi. If you do plan to use Wi-Fi, then this is not needed.

7. Plug the monitor into the wall outlet.

8. Plug the Raspberry Pi power adaptor into the wall outlet.

9. The final step, after everything else, is to plug the power supply into the Pi. The Raspberry Pi itself does not have a power switch, so applying power will start the boot process. If your power supply *does* come with a switch or button, then turn it on now.

At this point, your monitor will show a colorful "test pattern;" then clear the screen and show a number of raspberry icons at the top of the screen. After this, a bunch of status messages and texts may scroll up the screen.

First-Time Raspbian Setup

As mentioned earlier, we're going to be focusing on the Raspbian distribution from here out. Ubuntu MATE will be very similar, but not exactly the same, as what's shown here.

Assuming you got past the test pattern and the "raspberries," you'll wind up at the Raspbian welcome screen, as seen in Figure 1-3.

Figure 1-3. Welcome screen for Raspbian

Click "Next," and we'll get a localization screen that looks a lot like Figure 1-4.

Figure 1-4. *Localization settings*

Use the dropdown boxes to select your location as accurately as possible. This is used to set the time and determine what the various keys on your keyboard do. I once had a friend complain that Raspbian didn't work with any of his keyboards, as the punctuation keys were all wrong. Turned out, he had left the following dialog set to a UK keyboard, and he was in the United States. It's not all the same!

Now it's time to change the password for the default user, as shown in Figure 1-5. It might be useful to know if you don't change it here, the default is user "**pi**" and that user's password is "**raspberry**." Since this is the same username and password for every default Raspbian install, everywhere, it's a *very* good idea to change the password. This user has superuser access and has the ability to delete and change literally anything, so make the password something hard to guess.

Welcome to Raspberry Pi   _ □ ✕

Change Password

The default 'pi' user account currently has the password 'raspberry'.
It is strongly recommended that you change this to a different
password that only you know.

Enter new password:

Confirm new password:

☑ Hide characters

Press 'Next' to activate your new password.

Back   Next

Figure 1-5. *Setting the root password*

We will investigate creating a separate, more personalized user
account later. If you are experienced with Linux, the Pi user is a root-level
account, so it's not really a good idea to use this account for everyday work.

The next screen, shown in Figure 1-6, pertains to your monitor and
screen resolution. The screens up to this point have been low resolution
and pretty plain, since everything is at the lowest resolution possible. If the
Raspbian desktop is currently filling your entire screen, then don't check
the box. If there's a black bar or border on the edges, then click the box, and
Raspbian will adjust your settings accordingly. Be aware that you will not
see anything happen until the installation is done and the system reboots.

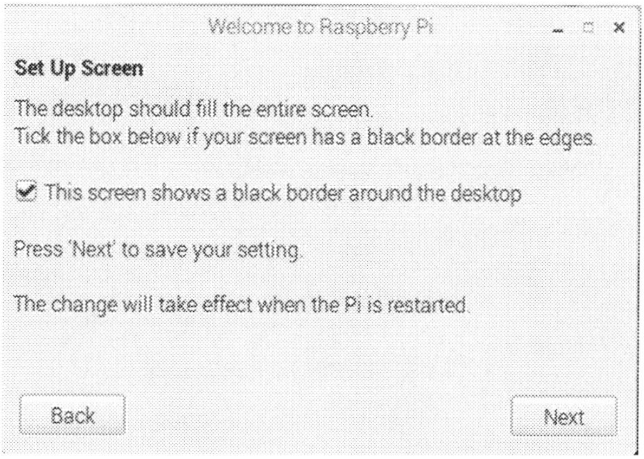

Figure 1-6. *Do you need screen resolution adjustments?*

Now, in Figure 1-7, it's time to set up your Wi-Fi network. If you are going to use Ethernet for your network, you can click "Skip." Otherwise, find your network here. Note that the Pi model 3B+ has both 2.4GHz and 5.0GHz capabilities available to you, while the regular non-plus model 3B and all the older models can only access 2.4GHz networks. Click the network you want to connect to, and then enter the password for the network on the following screen:

Figure 1-7. *Setting the Wi-Fi password*

After this, we are essentially done with the installation. The next and final screen, similar to Figure 1-8, will give us the opportunity to download updates and patches to software that didn't make it into the release on our SD card. You *can* skip this if you're in a hurry, but it's always best to have a fully updated system.

Figure 1-8. Let the updates begin!

If you choose to let it do the updates, you'll eventually get a dialog telling you your "System is up to date." At this point, you'll need to reboot the system, and everything should be ready to go.

It's safe at this stage to explore the menus and try out a few apps. Figure 1-9 shows a shot of LibreOffice Writer, the File Manager app, and the Chromium browser, all of which are already installed. Can you find them in the menus?

Hint   The Raspberry icon in the top-left corner is essentially Raspbian's version of the "Start" button for the menuing system.

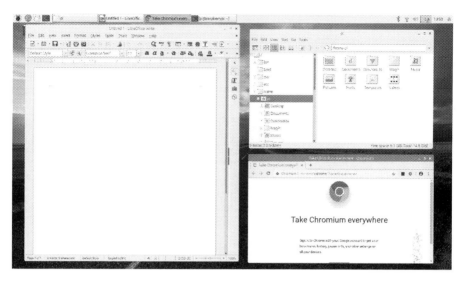

Figure 1-9. *LibreOffice, File Explorer, and Chromium come installed by default*

Conclusion

This chapter set the stage for the rest of the book. We bought and assembled all the pieces, and then we downloaded and created out boot media. We then went through the setup menus and ended up with a bare-bones but still fully working little computer. Feel free to poke around in the menus and run the apps, and see what it can do. If your needs are simple, such as just web browsing and email, you may already have all you need in a computer. More likely, you'll need to install a bunch of apps to do the things you want to do with the RPi. If you want to use your Raspberry Pi as a normal desktop computer, then you're good to go. Still, there are other ways of accessing the computer than just sitting in front of a monitor, as we'll see in the next chapter.

CHAPTER 2

Accessing and Configuring the Pi

In this chapter, we'll look at the various ways you can access your Pi computer, locally, remotely through the terminal, or by using a remote desktop. Finally, we'll look at adding new user accounts and setting up external hard drives and storage devices.

Using the GUI Desktop Locally

If you just turn on the Raspberry Pi after a default installation, you will be presented with the Raspbian desktop. It looks something like the MacOS or the Windows desktops, so you should find it somewhat intuitive to use. We will discuss using the desktop in detail in Chapter 3.

If all you're going to do is use the Pi as a desktop computer, that's fine, but one of the primary focuses of this book is how to use the command line to get things done. Before you can learn about the command line, you'll have to actually be able to get to one. There are three ways to do this, each one with increasing complexity and options.

© Brian Schell 2019
B. Schell, *Computing with the Raspberry Pi*, https://doi.org/10.1007/978-1-4842-5293-2_2

19

A Command Line on the Desktop

You can simply open a terminal window from the graphical user interface
(GUI) desktop. On the menu bar at the top of the screen, there's a gray
terminal icon. There's also a shortcut in the Raspberry ➤ Accessories
menu for the terminal. Click either of these, and you'll see a familiar-
looking black terminal with some text in it. This is quick and easy and
especially good if you do most of your work on the desktop.

Booting Directly to a Command Line

If you don't want to use the desktop, and you want to do *all* your work from
the command line, "*old school*," you can set Raspbian to simply boot to the
command line, just like in the olden days before GUIs took over. There are
two ways to make this happen.

First, under the Raspberry ➤ Preferences menu is an option for
"Raspberry Pi Configuration." This dialog has lots of useful things you can
change, but the one we're interested in right now is the third line, "Boot:"

You have the choice of booting "To Desktop" or "To CLI." The CLI is
the command-line interface. Click this option and then choose OK. On the
next reboot, you'll start at a command prompt.

Second, and probably the better choice, is to open a terminal window
and type sudo raspi-config in it. This is the text-based configuration
tool, and it has options that the previous tool doesn't. It's shown in
Figure 2-1. You can explore the various options in this extremely powerful
configuration tool when you have time, but for right now, we want to pick
line "3 Boot Options."

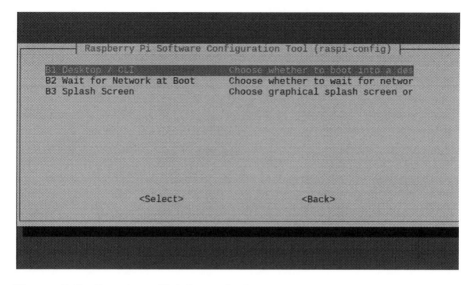

Figure 2-1. *Raspi-config's boot choices*

You'll want the first option, "Choose whether to boot into a desktop or not."

You will see four choices:

1. Text console, requiring user to log in

2. Text console, automatically logged in as "pi" user

3. Desktop GUI requiring user to log in

4. Desktop GUI automatically logged in a "pi" user

Choose option 1 and then choose "Finish." It will ask if you want to reboot now. Choose "Yes." The Pi reboots, and you should no longer see the desktop, just the black terminal screen with a prompt. On my screen, all I see is

```
Raspian GNU/Linux 9 raspberrypi tty1
Raspberrypi login:
```

Use the username "pi" or your regular username if you have set up an account for it. Then use the appropriate password to log in. You'll see the date of the last login, some generic copyright stuff, and the command prompt.

Note   Eventually, you may want to turn the desktop back on. If so, run sudo `raspi-config` again and choose option 3 to put things back the way they were.

Remote Terminal Access

You can also use some other computer or device to access the shell on the Raspberry Pi from somewhere else on your network. To set this up, run sudo `raspi-config` as before, and this time, choose "5 Interfacing Options" and then pick the second option under that menu, "SSH." This will enable (or disable) remote command-line access to your Pi with SSH (Secure **Sh**ell) protocol.

When you've done that, exit out of raspi-config and type `ifconfig` on the terminal. You'll see something similar to the following:

```
eth0: flags=4099<UP,BROADCAST,MULTICAST> mtu 1500
ether b8:27:eb:d1:6a:11 txqueuelen 1000 (Ethernet)
RX packets 0 bytes 0 (0.0 B)
RX errors 0 dropped 0 overruns 0 frame 0
TX packets 0 bytes 0 (0.0 B)
TX errors 0 dropped 0 overruns 0 carrier 0 collisions 0

lo: flags=73<UP,LOOPBACK,RUNNING> mtu 65536
inet 127.0.0.1 netmask 255.0.0.0
inet6 ::1 prefixlen 128 scopeid 0x10<host>
loop txqueuelen 1000 (Local Loopback)
```

```
RX packets 8 bytes 480 (480.0 B)
RX errors 0 dropped 0 overruns 0 frame 0
TX packets 8 bytes 480 (480.0 B)
TX errors 0 dropped 0 overruns 0 carrier 0 collisions 0

wlan0: flags=4163<UP,BROADCAST,RUNNING,MULTICAST> mtu 1500
inet 192.168.0.12 netmask 255.255.255.0 broadcast 192.168.0.255
inet6 fe80::faf9:e687:a474:6485 prefixlen 64 scopeid 0x20<link>
ether b8:27:eb:84:3f:44 txqueuelen 1000 (Ethernet)
RX packets 176596 bytes 109274663 (104.2 MiB)
RX errors 0 dropped 3 overruns 0 frame 0
TX packets 136755 bytes 140698474 (134.1 MiB)
TX errors 0 dropped 0 overruns 0 carrier 0 collisions 0
```

This command can tell you a lot about your network interfaces. You probably have three: *eth0* (Ethernet), *lo* (local), and *wlan* (wireless lan). Each of these that are in use will have an IP number on the second line of that interface's description (right after "inet"). For example, "lo" always has an IP of 127.0.0.1. If you are using Ethernet or Wi-Fi, then there will be a similar set of four numbers and periods for one or both of those interfaces. This is the IP address of your Raspberry Pi; it's how you find the right device on your network.

This is all you need.

Go to some other computer or device with a terminal app, and type

```
ssh pi@192.168.0.17
```

while substituting your IP number for mine. If everything is good, it should ask for your password. Enter it, and bang! You're on the command line inside your Pi. If this works, you have the option of leaving your Pi turned on and never using the monitor again—you *could* do all your computing remotely. Figure 2-2 is a screenshot of my iPad logged into my Pi using the *Blink* app.

```
blink> ssh pi@192.168.0.17
Password:
Linux raspberrypi 4.14.98-v7+ #1200 SMP Tue Feb 12 20:27:48 GMT 2019 armv7l

The programs included with the Debian GNU/Linux system are free software;
the exact distribution terms for each program are described in the
individual files in /usr/share/doc/*/copyright.

Debian GNU/Linux comes with ABSOLUTELY NO WARRANTY, to the extent
permitted by applicable law.
Last login: Wed May  8 14:38:39 2019 from 192.168.0.2
pi@raspberrypi:~ $ ls
Desktop  Documents  Downloads  MagPi  Music  Pictures  Public  Templates  Videos
pi@raspberrypi:~ $ █
```

Figure 2-2. *Accessing the Raspberry Pi from another computer, in this case an iPad*

Yes, I'm using a $1000 iPad Pro to access a $35 computer. Crazy? Probably!

Remote GUI Access

You can use the Raspberry Pi GUI desktop environment pretty much like any other computer; you sit in front of the monitor and use the mouse and keyboard that interface with the Pi. However, it's also very easy to set up the Pi so that you can access that GUI remotely. This means that you can access the Raspbian desktop from a laptop running Windows or Mac, or even from an iPad or mobile device, without a lot of work. Logging in through the text-mode SSH, as described in the previous section, is really powerful, but sometimes you just need the graphical user interface. This is easier than you might expect. Once you get everything set up, you can even disconnect your monitor, mouse, and keyboard and use the Pi "headless" by remoting in one way or the other.

From the terminal or command line, type

```
sudo raspi-config
```

as before, and this time, choose "5 Interfacing Options" and the third option under that menu, "VNC." This will enable (or disable) remote desktop access to your Pi with the VNC (**V**irtual **N**etwork **C**omputer) protocol. If you didn't already turn on SSH in the previous section, then you'll need to do that here now as well.

From a terminal window or command line, type the following commands:

```
sudo apt install tightvncserver
tightvncserver
```

This installs the TightVNC Server app, which handles logins and everything else for us on the Pi side of this project.

Tightvncserver will ask you to create a password for VNC. This password is only used for VNC connections, and it can be the same or different from your regular password; that's up to you. It will then ask if you want to create a view-only password. You can answer no to that part, as we don't need that. Next, you're ready to start the VNC server:

```
vncserver :1 -geometry 1920x1080 -depth 24
```

At first, just use this line without changing anything. Later, you may choose to modify this line to get more customized results. The *:1* parameter sets this up as screen number 1. You can set up multiple screens and switch between them or run them in separate windows on your client computer. If you aren't planning on doing this, just leave it at 1. The *-geometry 1920x1080* parameter is the screen resolution for our "virtual" desktop, and *-depth 24* sets the color palette so it looks good.

Again, these can all be experimented with and modified without harm, but start with these numbers for now.

Lastly, run `ifconfig` from the terminal to get the Pi's IP address, just like we did in the previous section.

Now it's time to go to your *other* computer. Bring up a web browser and download the RealVNC app (just the Viewer app; you don't need the server) from `www.realvnc.com/en/connect/download/viewer/`. They make versions for Windows, Mac, Linux, Android, iOS, Chromebooks, and a bunch of other platforms—just choose the right one for your system. It's completely free, so if you wind up on a page that wants you to purchase something, you've chosen the wrong option.

Once it's downloaded and installed, run RealVNC Viewer and accept the defaults. In the bar at the top, enter the IP number of the Pi followed by a colon and then the *number of the screen* you want to connect to, for example, `192.168.0.12:1` to connect to screen number 1 on the computer located at the IP address 192.168.0.12.

A warning about an unencrypted connection will appear. As long as you are connecting within your local network, this is fine. If you are trying to connect through the Internet, you may want to look into an encrypted connection method. You'll be asked for your password, and after that, you should see your Raspberry Pi desktop appear on your screen. Follow along with any onscreen tutorials that the RealVNC Viewer offers—there are ways to right-click, double-click, scroll, and all that, even if you're using a non-mouse device like an iPad.

VNC to access the GUI desktop and SSH to access the command line are powerful tools for working with the Raspberry Pi. At this stage, if you want to disconnect the Pi's keyboard, mouse, and monitor, you have the option to use it "headless." Since it connects to your network wirelessly, the only cable that you still need to have plugged in now is the power (and Ethernet if you need it). Of course, this is all optional. You'll get much faster performance with the desktop by using your Pi locally rather than through VNC, although the speed difference with SSH and the command line is negligible.

Create a New User Account

So far, we've used the default user, "pi," to log in. That's fine for someone who is using the Pi as a hobbyist device for electronics projects, but to use a Pi as a *computer*, we'll need to be doing lots more online, so better security is called for. Here's how to create a new user with whatever name you like, and, optionally, give them the ability to use *sudo* to perform superuser tasks.

Like all command-line work, this can be done locally on a monitor in front of your Pi or while logged in remotely with SSH or VNC; Linux doesn't distinguish between the two uses. You will need to be on a command line for this.

Use the *adduser* command to add a new user to your system:

```
sudo adduser username
```

Be sure to replace *username* with the user that you want to create.

You will be prompted to enter a password for this new user. A strong password is highly recommended!

```
Enter new UNIX password:
Retype new UNIX password:
passwd: password updated successfully
```

Follow the prompts to set the new user's information. It is fine to accept the defaults, leaving all of this information blank if you wish:

```
Changing the user information for username
Enter the new value, or press Enter for the default
    Full Name:
    Room Number:
    Work Phone:
    Home Phone:
    Other:
Is the information correct? Y/n
```

Now you have a standard Linux user account, with a home directory of its own, and everything that comes installed by default for a Linux user. This user cannot install or remove software or do other tasks with security restrictions. This is for safety and security reasons; you don't want to be able to accidentally delete important system files or apps.

In order to allow this user to do those restricted things, the user needs to be added to the "sudo group."

Use the *usermod* command to add the user to the sudo group:

```
sudo usermod -aG sudo username
```

By default, members of the sudo group have sudo privileges.

Use the *su* command (switch user) to switch to the new user account:

```
Su - username
```

As the new user, verify that you can use sudo by attempting to update the Linux repositories:

```
sudo apt update
```

If there are messages involving "permission denied," go back and try again. If there are no messages, then everything worked as it should.

Now, anytime you want to run a command with superuser privileges, just prepend "sudo" to the command that you want to run:

```
sudo command_to_run
```

For example, you can list the contents of the /root directory, which is normally only accessible to the root user:

```
sudo ls -al /root
```

You will be prompted for the password of the user account the first time you use *sudo* in a session.

Setting Up External Storage

So far, we've booted and run our operating system from the little SD card. The problem with SD cards is that they are slow and less than super-reliable. I've gone through several that simply stopped working. On the other hand, I know people who swear by them, so your mileage may vary, but I prefer to store important data on an actual hard drive. Once the hard drive is set up, we can even boot from it if we choose, leaving that SD card in the dust!

There are a few things to consider before going too deep with external drives. You would expect that adding an external hard drive or SSD drive would make everything run faster, but this is not necessarily the case. The way the Pi is designed requires it to search for an operating system on the SD card slot first, then detect the hard drive, and then boot from the hard drive if there isn't an SD card; and all this searching takes time. What this translates to is that boot time will be *slower* using an external drive than the SD card.

Another consideration is that the interface used by the USB controller is shared with that used by the Ethernet controller. This means that heavy I/O through the USB ports can slow down network access and vice versa. There's no way to predict exactly how much this will impact speed, but there *is* an impact.

That said, normal apps that access the disk heavily *should* run faster. And no matter how speed is impacted, spinning hard drives and SSD drives will both be much *safer* places to store important data than the easily corruptible SD card.

The first step is deciding whether you want to be able to boot from the hard drive or if you just want to use it as a data drive. If you want to boot from the hard drive, then continue here; if not, you can skip ahead to the next section.

Setting Up a Hard Drive for Booting

Note that this process requires a fresh install of your Raspberry Pi's operating system onto the hard drive. **Whatever is currently on the hard drive will be erased.**

Note   At the time of this writing, the Raspberry Pi model 4 has been available for around a month. As of right now, the Pi model 4 *cannot* boot from a hard drive; they must boot from the SD card. This limitation is expected to be corrected fairly soon in a future update, but as of autumn 2019, this is an issue to be dealt with.

This process can be done using either old-style spinning hard drives or SSD technology, and even a USB flash drive is an option. Be careful with hard drives that are powered through USB—the Pi is a very low-power device, and it may not be able to handle powering the drive as well as the computer. For best results, use a hard drive that is externally powered—one that comes with an AC adaptor or "wall wart." I've also found that this process depends a lot on how the external drive is designed—I have tried several that just will not allow booting at all, but then work just fine for data storage.

1.   Go back to your regular computer; download and install Etcher from Balena.io just as we did when setting up the SD card. You may already have this read to go from before.

2.   Plug your external hard drive into your computer.

3.   Choose your Raspbian image (or whichever distribution you are using) in the left box, choose the new hard drive in the center box, and hit

"Flash!" when you're ready to start, just like before.
Etcher may give you a warning about the drive being
"an unusually large size." This is simply pointing out
that we're not using the expected SD card anymore.
Just make sure you're formatting the *correct* drive
before hitting "Flash."

4. Essentially, this process is exactly the same as
   copying the operating system to the SD card, only
   now we're doing it with a computer. It's *exactly* the
   same process.

5. When the flashing is done, disconnect the drive
   from your computer and plug it into your Pi.

If you have a Raspberry Pi model 3B+, then you can remove the SD
card, turn on the power, and the Pi should boot right up. You're done!

If you have a Raspberry Pi model 2 or 3B (not the 3B+ or 4), then you
have some additional steps:

6. Leave your old SD card plugged in for the moment,
   as we'll still need it this one last time to boot.

7. Turn on power to the Pi, and let it boot up.

8. Get to a terminal and type

   ```
   sudo nano /boot/config.txt
   ```

   This will bring up the Nano editor, which we have
   not discussed yet, but is pretty straightforward to
   use. Move your cursor down to the bottom of this
   file and add the following:

   ```
   program_usb_boot_mode=1
   ```

To save the file with Nano, press `Ctrl-o` and then `Ctrl-x` to exit.

9. Reboot the Pi, still with the SD card in it.

10. Type the following:

    `vcgencmd otp_dump | grep 17:`

    If you see the value `17:3020000a`, then it's all good.

11. Turn off the Pi, remove the SD card, restore power, and see what happens: your Pi should boot right up from the hard drive.

Note that this is a relatively new feature with the Raspberry Pi, and it *does not always work* with every external drive. If you are planning on purchasing a new hard drive for your Pi, do a little online research to see if that specific model is known to work or not.

Adding an External Hard Drive for Data

Surprisingly, it's easier to make a boot disk than a blank drive, since Etcher does all the work for us. Preparing an external data drive involves a bit more work. This section will end with a hard drive which will mount automatically when you boot the Pi and can be used for your data files and optionally your /home directory. If you already have a Linux-formatted (i.e., *ext4*) drive with important data already on it that you wish to use as a data drive, you can skip to step 15. If you have a blank drive, or want to re-task a drive with "junk" already on it, then start right here:

1. Plug in the hard drive to power (if necessary) and to the Raspberry Pi. Power up the Raspberry Pi and boot from the SD card as always.

2. Bring up a terminal window and type

    ```
    sudo fdisk /dev/sda
    ```

    Because you are using the *fdisk* command in
    superuser mode (sudo), it will ask for your password.
    After you enter the password, you should see

    ```
    Welcome to fdisk (util-linux 2.29.2)
    Changes will remain in memory only, until you decide to
    write them. Be careful before using the write command.
    ```

    ```
    Command (m for help):
    ```

    fdisk is a very powerful tool for creating, deleting,
    partitioning, and otherwise changing hard drive
    attributes. If you are curious about the options, press
    m to see the menu choices.

3. Press p to *print* the partition table. The numbers will
    probably be somewhat different, but should look
    something like this:

    ```
    Command (m for help): p
    Disk /dev/sda: 698.7 GiB, 750156374016 bytes,
    1465149168 sectors
    Units: sectors of 1 * 512 = 512 bytes
    Sector size (logical/physical): 512 bytes / 512 bytes
    I/O size (minimum/optimal): 512 bytes / 512 bytes
    Disklabel type: dos
    Disk identifier: 0x43c1e3bb
    ```

    ```
    Device    Boot Start      End  Sectors  Size Id Type
    /dev/sda1        8192    96042    87851 42.9M  c W95 FAT32 (LBA)
    /dev/sda2       98304 10551295 10452992    5G 83 Linux
    ```

    ```
    Command (m for help):
    ```

From this, I can see that my drive is 698.7GB and is currently set up with two partitions, */dev/sda1* and */dev/sda2*. We don't need to worry about most of the other information for now. Our goal here is to delete those old partitions and create a single large partition to replace them.

4. Press d for "delete partition":

   `Partition number (1,2, default 2):`

   Again, you may only have one partition or more than two or maybe none at all. The goal here is to delete all the partitions. I will enter 2 to delete the second partition; then I will hit d again and enter 1 to delete the first partition.
   After all the partitions are gone, use the p command to print the partition table again. If the previous step worked correctly, there shouldn't be anything listed after "Disk identifier." The two */sda* devices should be gone. Again, if you have a new, blank drive, you may not have seen any partitions at all.

5. Use the n command in fdisk to create a new partition.

6. Unless you know some reason to do otherwise, choose p to make the new partition *Primary*.

7. Make the new partition "Partition 1" by pressing 1 or hitting the enter key for the default.

8. Accept the default values for the first and last sectors. This will make the new partition fill the entire hard drive.

9. It may take a few seconds, but you should soon see

    ```
    Created a new partition 1 of type 'Linux' and of
    size 698.7 GiB.
    ```

    Assuming the size given approximates the size of your hard drive, you're doing good. If for some reason you want to make multiple partitions, you can adjust the previous few steps to accommodate your needs.

10. When you are done creating partitions, use the w command in fdisk to write changes to the disk. Nothing you have done so far is permanent until you do this. Once you write your changes, all data, partitions, and everything else will be wiped from the disk; so be sure everything looks good before you commit to this.

11. Press p to once again print the list of partitions. It should now look somewhat like this:

    ```
    Command (m for help): p
    Disk /dev/sda: 698.7 GiB, 750156374016 bytes,
    1465149168 sectors
    Units: sectors of 1 * 512 = 512 bytes
    Sector size (logical/physical): 512 bytes / 512 bytes
    I/O size (minimum/optimal): 512 bytes / 512 bytes
    Disklabel type: dos
    Disk identifier: 0x43c1e3bb

    Device    Boot Start        End    Sectors   Size Id Type
    /dev/sda1      2048 1465149167 1465147120 698.7G 83 Linux

    Command (m for help):
    ```

And as you see near the bottom, there is a new device, */dev/sda1*, that uses the entire hard drive.

12.   We're done with fdisk, so use the q command to quit.

13.   You will need to reboot the Pi for changes to take effect.

14.   The new hard drive now has an empty, unformatted partition, but it's not good for anything until we format it. Type

```
sudo mkfs /dev/sda1
```

This will format the drive with a Linux file system. Depending on the size and speed of the drive, this will take some time, but you should be able to watch the progress onscreen.

15.   Now that the hard drive is partitioned and formatted, you will need to create a *mount point* within your regular directory structure. You can put it wherever you want, but I generally just put it in the / (root) directory. Type

```
sudo mkdir /mydrive
```

This will create a new directory called "mydrive" in the / directory. Next, the physical hard drive needs to be "mounted" to that mount point. Assuming your hard drive was called *sda1* back in step 11, then you would type the following:

```
sudo mount /dev/sda1 /mydisk
```

Of course, if your disk is something other than /dev/sda1, or if you used something other than /mydisk, then you should make the appropriate substitutions in the preceding command.

16. Depending on what you plan to do with the external drive, you may need to set ownership of the new drive to your user account (instead of root). For example, since I plan to do most things under the username "*brian*," I will need to change ownership of the drive to that user:

```
sudo chown brian:brian -R /mydisk
```

And now the user *brian* can save and manipulate files in the drive without needing to use sudo all the time.

17. Test out everything by typing the following:

```
cd /mydisk
touch test.txt
ls
```

The *touch* command simply changes the file date on an existing file or creates a new, blank file if it doesn't already exist. The *ls* command is for "list structure," the Linux way of showing the files in a directory. It should list

```
lost+found.  test.txt
```

Lost+found is something that is always generated automatically, but *test.txt* is the file that you just created with the *touch* command. If you see it, then you should be able to save, copy, delete, and otherwise manipulate files within the new drive.

Setting Up the External Drive to Mount Automatically

If you plan to use the Raspbian desktop only, then this section is unnecessary, as the desktop will automatically mount any hard drive that is plugged in. On the other hand, if you plan to boot directly into the command line, then you will need to manually set the system up to automatically mount the external drive. Either way, it doesn't hurt to set up the drive to automatically mount itself:

1. Type

   ```
   sudo fdisk -l
   ```

   This will list all the various partitions and disks that are available to you. Usually, the external drive will be at the bottom of the list. You need to make note of the "Device" name, for example, /**dev**/**sda1** or /**dev**/ **sda2** or whatever comes up if you have more than one drive or partition connected.

2. We will now modify one of the main Linux configuration files to recognize the drive at boot-up time. We will edit the /*etc/fstab* file using the Nano editor. Type

   ```
   sudo nano /etc/fstab
   ```

   You'll see something similar to the following:

```
proc                    /proc  proc  defaults         0  0
PARTUUID=af2d9ccc-01    /boot  vfat  defaults         0  2
PARTUUID=af2d9ccc-02    /      ext4  defaults,noatime 0  1
# a swapfile is not a swap partition, no line here
#   use  dphys-swapfile swap[on|off]  for that
```

The PARTUUID numbers will certainly be different from these, but the file should otherwise resemble this closely. Move the cursor to the end of the file and add

```
/dev/sda1 /mydisk ext4 defaults,nofail 0 0
```

substituting */dev/sda1* and */mydisk* with whatever you used. Use Ctrl-o to save and then Ctrl-x to exit Nano. Once you reboot, the new hard drive should be available to you to use automatically, whether on the command line or desktop, every time you boot the Pi.

Moving Your Home Directory to an External Drive

Most operations in Linux perform operations on your own data files, which are almost always stored somewhere beneath the */home* directory on your disk. By default, /home is created on the SD card when the operating system is installed, and each user's own home directory is created beneath it when the user is created. The problem with this system is that if you are booting from the SD card, you may not want to save all your data files on that SD card. Probably just the opposite, since that's the reason you installed an external hard drive. Fortunately, there is an easy procedure that allows you to move your entire */home* structure to an external drive.

You need to have root privileges to do all this. We'll be using *sudo* to give ourselves the privileges we need. By prepending *sudo* in front of a command, we run that command as a superuser (sudo = "Super User DO ___"). You need to be extra cautious when using *sudo*, as you can delete just about anything or cause no end to your problems with a typo.

1. Start by making sure your external drive is connected and then open a terminal. There's a good chance that your hard drive will auto-mount when you plug it in, but for this procedure, you'll need to make sure your drive is **not** mounted. To unmount it, type

    ```
    sudo umount /mydisk
    ```

2. Next, mount your new partition in a *temporary* location:

    ```
    sudo mkdir /media/tmp
    sudo mount -t ext4 /media/tmp
    ```

3. This will mount the external hard drive at */media/tmp* for now.

4. Navigate to your root folder:

    ```
    cd /home
    ```

5. Copy all your data recursively, including hidden files:

    ```
    sudo cp -rp ./ /media/tmp
    ```

6. Once all the files are finished copying, you can move the home directory and mount the new one. Make sure no program is currently using the home directory, or you will get errors.

    ```
    sudo umount /media/tmp
    sudo rm -rf /media/tmp
    ```

    This gets rid of the tmp folder mount point, which is no longer necessary; it does *not* erase your data. All the data from your old /home directory is now safely on the hard drive.

    ```
    sudo mv /home /oldhome
    ```

This moves the original /home folder that points to the SD card and makes room for a "new" /home folder.

```
sudo mkdir /home
```

This creates a new mount point called /home.

Note that the following should all be entered as a single line. There isn't room to show it unbroken:

```
sudo echo "/dev/sda1 /home ext4
defaults,noatime,nodiratime 0 0" >> /etc/fstab
```

This changes *the /etc/fstab* file, which tells the operating system what to do with hard drives, to support the new drive.

Again, you should replace */dev/sda1* with your drive and partition info.
Now we can test it by mounting /home:

```
sudo mount /home
```

If this doesn't work, go back and review your steps. After you have confirmed everything is working and copied over, and you don't need your old home directory anymore, you can delete it from the SD card:

```
sudo rm -fr /oldhome
```

And that's it. It's a lot of steps, but now all your work will be permanently and safely stored on your hard drive instead of the SD card.

Back Up and Restore Your SD Card

By this point, you've put a lot of work into getting your Raspberry Pi computer all set up. You've got Wi-Fi passwords entered, you have an external drive configured, and maybe you've moved your home directory to that hard drive. If you've been able to go the extra step and make your system boot from the hard drive, your system should be as safe and reliable as any other computer.

Unfortunately, for many people, booting from a hard drive is not an option—many drives still don't support it. In this case, you will still need to continue booting your system from the SD card, but at least you can keep your important data on an external hard drive. It's not a perfect solution, but it's very workable. In this case, the weak point is still the SD card—they do tend to get corrupted from time to time. Once in a while, it's a good idea to make a backup of the SD card that contains your operating system and all the apps and configuration data stored in it. That way, if something does corrupt the card, you can just restore your configured settings and system right over it, and since your personal data will be stored on the hard drive, nothing important will be lost.

To back up the SD card, you will once again need another computer, along with whatever adaptor you may need to plug the SD card into it.

Shut down your Raspberry Pi using the following command:

```
sudo shutdown
```

And when everything stops, turn off the power to the Pi. Next, remove the SD card and move it to your computer for the next steps.

From a Mac:

1. Bring up a terminal window, but do not plug in the SD card yet.

2. Type

   ```
   diskutil list
   ```

3. Insert the SD card.

4. Now type that same command again

    ```
    diskutil list
    ```

    and note the new drive name that appears. This is the SD card name/number.

5. In the terminal, type the following, replacing the x in *rdiskx* with whatever the disk number is that you found in step 6:

    ```
    sudo dd if=/dev/rdiskx of=./backup_file.dmg
    ```

6. This can take a very long time (my card took nearly an hour), and there is no feedback from the program. Be patient!

Someday, if you need to restore the card:

1. Figure out the disk number by repeating steps 1–4 mentioned earlier.

2. Type the following, replacing rdiskx with whatever your SD card's drive is called:

    ```
    diskutil unmountDisk /dev/rdiskx
    sudo dd if=./backup_file.dmg of=/dev/rdiskx
    sudo diskutil eject /dev/rdiskx
    ```

From Windows:

3. Download and install the **Win32DiskImager** app from https://sourceforge.net/projects/win32diskimager/files/latest/download.

4. Insert the SD card.

5. Run Win32DiskImager, and then choose both the
    location where you want to create the backup file
    and the name of the SD card. Again, it is important
    to make sure you are writing to the correct drive;
    choosing the wrong drive can be disastrous—you
    could accidentally overwrite your Window drive or
    important data, so double-check that you're writing
    to the drive you intend to erase.

6. Click "Read" to begin copying.

7. This can take a very long time, but you can watch
    the progress bar as shown in Figure 2-3.

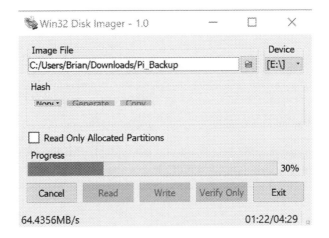

Figure 2-3. Win32DiskImager reading the SD card

If at some point you need to restore the SD card from your backup, just
run Win32DiskImager, choose the backup file and the SD card drive letter,
and choose "Write" instead of "Read" in the preceding steps to the process
in reverse.

Conclusion

By now, you've got a fully working computer in front of you that runs a full version of Raspbian Linux. You can make it boot to the desktop or command line and even save files on an external drive if you want.

In the next chapter, we'll look at what's special about the Raspbian GUI desktop and how we can customize it and configure it the way we want. After that, we'll start installing apps!

CHAPTER 3

The Raspberry Pi Desktop Tools

Your Raspberry Pi-based computer is now all assembled and working. Now what? It's time to learn how to use the basic user interface. If you've ever used Windows or a Mac, you already know how the mouse and keyboard work, but the menus and controls in Raspbian are a little different. We'll also spend some time explaining several different ways that software and apps can be installed, and this is significantly different from other operating systems, so you'll absolutely need take a few notes here.

Using the Interface

Now that we have all the hardware set up, it's time to look at software. Once you've gone through all the system setup screens, you'll be presented with a blank desktop environment, as shown in Figure 3-1.

© Brian Schell 2019
B. Schell, *Computing with the Raspberry Pi*, https://doi.org/10.1007/978-1-4842-5293-2_3

Figure 3-1. *The Raspbian desktop*

There are several important sections to note. At the top of the screen is the menu bar, and there are groups of icons on the left and the right. The three icons next to the raspberry (see Figure 3-2) are for the Chromium web browser (the globe icon), the File Manager (the file folders icon), and the terminal (the command prompt icon). If you don't remember what these are, you can just hover your mouse over them, and little "tool tips" will appear.

Figure 3-2. *The upper-left icon area*

Beneath the raspberry icon is an icon for the trash can, and, if you plugged in an external hard drive, one or more hard drive icons should appear here.

At the top right of the screen, as in Figure 3-3, are the hardware controller buttons.

Figure 3-3. *The upper-right icon area*

These buttons allow you to control Bluetooth (the Bluetooth logo), Wi-Fi and Ethernet (the up/down arrows), and the audio volume (the speaker icon).

Next to that is a simple meter that shows how much CPU capacity is being used (in percent), followed by a clock/calendar, and lastly you will find an "eject button icon" that you can use to eject media such as flash drives and other removable media.

The list of installed apps can be accessed by clicking the raspberry icon at the top left. The menu options that have an arrow next to them have sub-menus that you can explore. For example, click the raspberry icon, then move your mouse down, and hover over the option for "Preferences"; and you'll get a list of apps that involve customizing the interface, just as in Figure 3-4.

Figure 3-4. *The Preferences menu options*

The last item on the list, "Theme and Appearance Settings," is worth taking a closer look at. This screen allows for some very fine-tuned interface options. You can change the font of the desktop, the style of the icons, and even the way all the dialogs look. For example, if you choose the "Adwaita-dark" theme under the "Widgets" tab, you effectively put the desktop into dark mode, as in Figure 3-5.

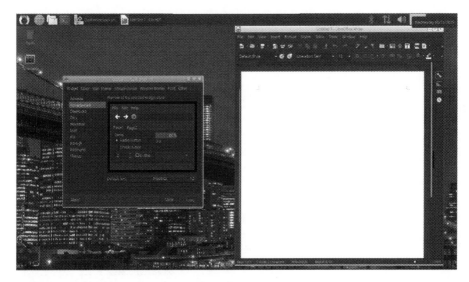

Figure 3-5. *Adwaita-dark theme for Widgets*

Under Preferences ➤ Desktop Preferences, you can change the colors of the menu bar; and under the "Desktop" tab, you can change the background picture, or if you don't want a background photo, you can choose a plain, single-color background.

Overall, you'll find that working with the Raspbian desktop is a lot like working with Windows or Mac in the way things work. Right-clicking the mouse or two-finger trackpad clicking will often bring up some kind of contextual menu, items can be dragged around the desktop, and cut and paste options work just about the same as they do on other systems.

Shutting Down the System

With most modern operating systems, you have to go through a "shutdown process" before you turn off your computer, and the Pi is no different. When you are ready to turn off (or reboot) your Raspberry Pi, you can do this from either the desktop or the command line.

From within the GUI, click the raspberry icon, and the last thing on the dropdown menu is "Shutdown." You'll see a dialog box with three choices: Shut Down, Reboot, and Cancel.

From the command line, you can simply type

```
sudo shutdown
```

or

```
sudo reboot
```

The File Manager

One system app that needs some discussion is the File Manager. This app is launched by clicking the file folder icon on the menu bar. This will bring up an app that looks very much like Windows' File Explorer or the Mac's Finder. See Figure 3-6.

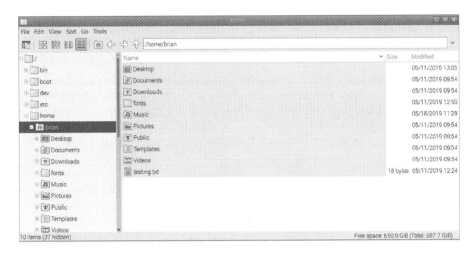

Figure 3-6. *The File Manager app*

The system file structure is displayed in the left pane, while the various folders and files show up in the right pane. Across the top is the menu bar. In the file structure pane, you can expand or collapse folders either by clicking the plus or minus signs next to the folder icons or by double-clicking them.

Keep in mind that if you are coming from a Windows background, the Linux file structure is very different from what you may be used to. You have full access (called permissions in Linux) to delete, copy, and manipulate most files within your own user account folder (called "brian" in the screenshot in Figure 3-6); but you cannot alter things outside that directory unless you use the sudo command. The only way to run a sudo command is to type it from the command line. This may seem like an annoyance, but it's a security feature that is time-tested in decades of Unix use.

Installing Apps

There are a lot of great apps already installed with Raspbian; there's an office app, a web browser, a media player, and a lot of other useful things.

If you haven't already, now would be a great time to browse through the menus and see what all is in there. Even with all that, the Raspbian folks obviously couldn't include *everything* out there, since Raspbian is essentially just a version of Linux, and there are a *vast* number of apps available for that. Once in a while, you'll hear about some great thing that didn't come included with Raspbian that you want to try.

There are three primary ways to install software on Raspbian: compiling it from source code, downloading it from the Ubuntu repositories, or installing it from the command line.

Building Apps from Source Code

This is the hardest way to do it, and unless you know what you're doing, I wouldn't go this route unless the software you want has very explicit instructions for building the app. Most Raspbian apps are open source software, meaning that you can actually download and read the programming code that went into making the software.

Some apps that are still in development only offer this source code, and the code has to be compiled in order to run. There are a lot of variables involved with available libraries, tools, and languages; so unless you just absolutely have to build the app, look for an easier way.

Installing Apps from the Add/Remove Software Tool

Knowing how hard it is to build software from source code, the folks who put together Raspbian created an app that would index and list hundreds of apps and tools that are ready to use, just like Raspbian's version of the app stores from other operating systems. This app can be found under Raspbian ➤ Preferences ➤ Add/Remove Software and can be seen in Figure 3-7.

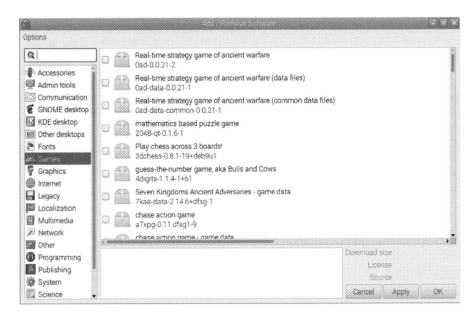

Figure 3-7. *Add/Remove Software tool*

You can browse the categories in the left pane and then scroll through the lists of apps in the right pane. If you know the specific name of something you want to install, type it in the search box. If you find an app that you want to try, select it and click *OK*. After a few moments, the app should be downloaded and installed for you. After an app has been installed, it will show up on this list with a checkmark next to it. If you uncheck the box and click "*Apply*," it will be uninstalled. Easy!

Even better, this tool allows you to easily look for and install updates and patches to the apps you've already installed. Click the options menu on the Add/Remove Software app. The first option is "Check for Updates." Click it, and you'll see something like Figure 3-8.

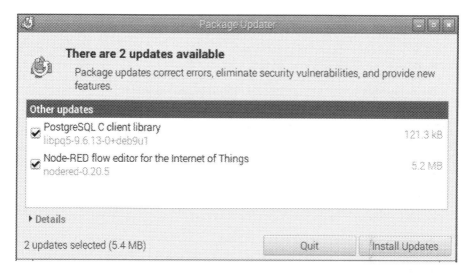

Figure 3-8. *Available Updates screen*

And here it's very clear that I have two apps that need updating. Click "Install Updates," and they'll download and install the updates for you.

There are two problems with this method. First, there's not much description of what everything is, so unless you have a specific app or tool in mind, you may never find it. Second, this tool doesn't work remotely. You can run the Add/Remove Software tool in VNC, but the software *will not* install. This may be a security feature, or it may be a bug, but it *will not* work.

Installing Apps from the Command Line

The Add/Remove Software tool that we just described is really easy to use, but you may soon find that the selection of apps is still somewhat limited. There's a lot of good stuff there, and I strongly recommend browsing and exploring those apps, but there are a huge number of very powerful apps that still aren't included in that list. I have found the command line is the easiest way to install just about anything I ever wanted. There's nothing complicated at all about this, but the one requirement is that you have to know the name of the package you want in advance. This requires some reading or some Internet research, but once you know *what* you want, getting it is easy.

First, launch a terminal window. Then, type the following lines:

```
sudo apt update
sudo apt install packagename
```

The first line updates all the *repositories*. These online repositories index all the available apps and tools that are available and the Internet locations that hold the install files for them. They change constantly with new versions and new tools being added all the time, so I always run this update command first, just to make sure the newest versions are found.

In the second line, *sudo* is once again the command that gives you superuser permissions, which is required to install software. *Apt* is short for *Advanced Packaging Tool*, and it is the app that does the installation. *Install* is what we specifically want the apt program to do, and *packagename* should be replaced with the name of the package we want to install.

For example, if you've been hearing about this neat app called *Neofetch*, you can just type

```
sudo apt install neofetch
```

to install it. If you later decide you don't want Neofetch anymore, you can delete it in a similar way:

```
sudo apt remove neofetch
```

Try it now. *Neofetch* is not installed on your Pi by default, so let's install it. Type the preceding commands to update the repositories, and then install the app. When that's done, type the command neofetch on the command line. You should see something very similar to Figure 3-9.

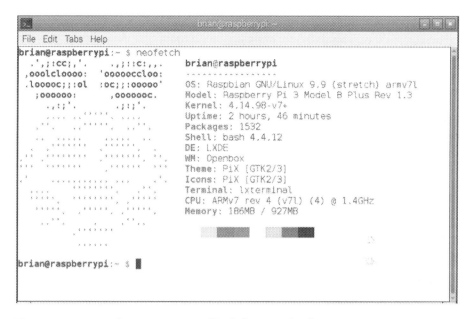

Figure 3-9. *We have just installed the Neofetch app*

Neofetch is a nice little command-line app that prints out the textual-graphic representation of the Raspbian logo and reports on some technical stuff about our little machine as well. It's not super useful, but it wasn't there before we installed it!

Every so often, you should update *all* your software. On a system like Windows, there are so many updates coming in so often that it quickly becomes a major hassle, but it's different on Linux. The Linux system will not automatically perform upgrades; you have to do it yourself, but at least you can do it when *you're* ready. This can be done with two commands:

```
sudo apt update
sudo apt upgrade
```

Again, the first line loads in a fresh list of repositories, and then the second line upgrades everything that has an available update.

Along the same lines is an enhanced version of this process that allows you to upgrade the ***entire operating system*** to the newest version of Raspbian Linux:

```
sudo apt update
sudo apt dist-upgrade
```

But be aware that you probably already have the latest full distribution of Raspbian—it may only be updated once or twice a year, so most of the time this won't do anything.

Note that there are also other ways of installing software from the command line. We looked at `apt` (**A**dvanced **P**ackaging **T**ool) earlier, but there are also `pip` (**P**ackage **I**nstaller for **P**ython) and `curl` (**C**opy from **URL**) that are also used occasionally. Which one you use depends on various factors: `pip` is used to install Python scripts, and `curl` is used to download and install directly over the Internet. The vast majority of apps install using `apt`, but be on the lookout for the occasional app that needs one of the others. Of course, I'll give the installation command for each app that we look at here.

OK, now we are able to search for, install, delete, and update software any which way we want using `apt`. Now it's time to get some work done!

Cleaning Up the Raspbian Menus

Raspbian installs many of the most common apps and tools that the Raspberry Pi Foundation believes people are most likely to use. The vast majority of people who buy a Pi are doing so to do electronics projects and experimenting. This means there are a lot of scientific, electronics, programming, and interfacing apps on the Pi; and we aren't going to want those at all in our "getting work done" desktop. We could go through and uninstall all of the things we don't want, but in some cases, these apps include files and libraries that may be used by other apps, and we don't want to cause problems by deleting the wrong things. So rather than uninstall them, we can simply remove them from the menus. The menu editor can be found under Raspberry ➤ Preferences ➤ Main Menu Editor.

Using this tool is pretty not complicated; just select a menu in the left pane and then "uncheck" apps on the right that you want to remove. If you find that you removed something important, just go back and check the box again—nothing is really deleted, although you have the option of deleting them if you want. You can also remove entire menus, such as "Programming" and "Education" as I have in the screenshot in Figure 3-10. You can also move individual apps up or down the list, add dividers, or move them to different menus if you choose. As you can see in Figure 3-10, it's a very easy, flexible system that can be configured to your specifications.

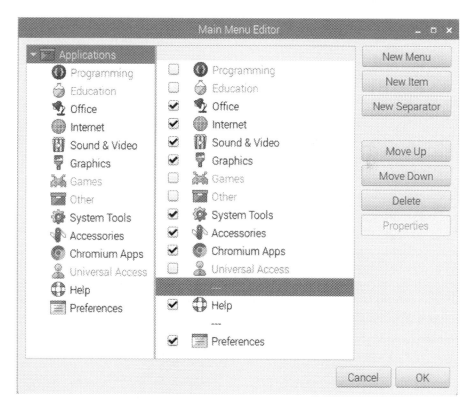

Figure 3-10. *Main Menu Editor—removing the unused items*

As a side note, it's probably a good idea to skim through all the menus and take a look at what's there. There are a number of apps that are already installed on your system, but their menu entries are already grayed out by default. If you want to try these apps, just turn them on and explore.

As we've seen, `sudo apt install appname` will not only install a new app, but it will most often create a menu item for the app as well. This isn't something you can always assume, and once in a while, you may install an app and not find it in the menus. In order to create a menu item, open the Main Menu Editor and click "New Item," and you'll see a small dialog that looks like Figure 3-11.

Figure 3-11. *Adding a new menu item*

This allows us to create a menu item for literally *anything*. Type in some text for the *Name* field and, optionally, the *Comment* field. Both of these can say anything you like. In the *Command* field, you have two choices: you can enter in the *exact* same text you would use to start an app on the command line, or you can click the button and browse to where the app is located in the file system. There's also a checkbox that lets you run the command in a terminal window. If you are running some kind of GUI app, then you don't need the terminal, but if you want to run a command-line app, then launching it in the terminal allows it to be interactive.

In addition, if you have an icon image that you would like to assign to this menu item, you can click the generic icon picture and choose a new one.

Let's take a common command-line action and make a menu item out of it. For our example, we know that sudo apt update is the command that updates your software repositories. It's common to do this before installing anything, just so you can be sure you are getting the newest version of the software. Still, you don't have to actually type that every time; you can make it a menu item.

To do this, you'd type

Update Repositories in the *Name* field

sudo apt update in the *Command* field

Update things before downloading a new app in the *Comment* field.

Lastly, you would want to see this command work and be alerted if there was an error, so you would check *Launch in Terminal*. Click OK, and now go look at the menu. You should see "Update Repositories" in the menu, similar to Figure 3-12.

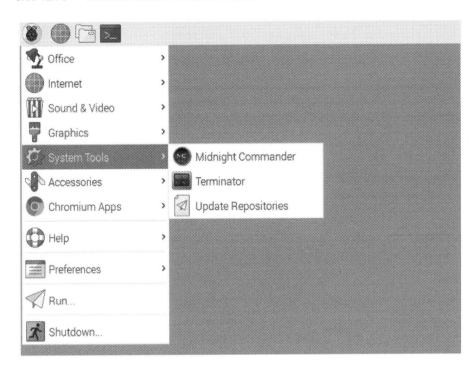

Figure 3-12.   *Update Repositories is now a menu item!*

Cloud Services

One thing that I've found incredibly useful over the years is making heavy use out of some kind of cloud syncing service. Dropbox, Google Drive, OneDrive, iCloud, and a dozen other options are available for Windows and Mac, but what's out there for our little Pi?

Well, there's bad news and there's good news. *None* of the major cloud storage providers have a native app that works on the Raspberry Pi. At one time, there was a workaround that allowed Dropbox to work, but Dropbox made changes that broke that. Insynchq.com makes a test version of their client that they claim will work, but I've never managed to get it to install properly. Keep an eye out for this; they may get it fully working someday.

In the meantime, all the major services *will* work through their respective web interfaces. It's not the same as having an integrated native app that will sync folders seamlessly in the background, but at least you can make use of your favorite service to upload and download files manually. As the RPi devices become more powerful, these providers will see the benefit of creating a native interface, so expect changes here.

Conclusion

Now you've gotten into the desktop interface, gone through the menus, and maybe customized a few of them; and more importantly, we learned several different methods of installing new apps, and we'll need all of them. One of the often-debated weaknesses of Linux is the complexity of installing software and apps, and the simple fact that we just looked at multiple ways to do it proves that true.

Still, we know how it's done now, so in the next chapter, we'll look at the best apps for the Raspberry Pi desktop.

## CHAPTER 4

The Raspberry Pi Desktop Apps

We've set up our equipment, and we've played with the basic desktop a bit; now it's time to get some actual work done. In this chapter, we'll go through an overview of all the best GUI desktop apps that you can use to get your work done. There's an office suite, numerous writing tools and email clients, choices of web browsers, notes apps, audio and video editing tools, illustration and graphic apps, and even some online file management tools.

Keep in mind that the intended audience of this book is normal, everyday users of desktop computers, not developers or engineers. There are a vast number of programming, coding, templating, and prototyping apps available for the Pi, as well as a very large number of engineering, electronics, and robotics apps that we will *not* be covering here. There are many other excellent books and web references on the more technical side of the Raspberry Pi if you need that.

Explanation of App Descriptions

Each app listed for the remainder of the book has a heading similar to the following:

Scribus Details:

© Brian Schell 2019
B. Schell, *Computing with the Raspberry Pi*, https://doi.org/10.1007/978-1-4842-5293-2_4

Installation: `sudo apt install scribus`

Menu location: `Raspberry Menu` ➤ `Graphics`

Help: `man scribus`

Web site: `www.scribus.net/`

Let's go through this step by step:

1. **Details:** First is the name of the app; in this case, it's called "Scribus."

2. **Installation:** The second line is the command line you need to type to install the app. Most of them use the "sudo apt install <name>" format that we've discussed before, but some require something else. Occasionally, a more complex installation will refer you to the text or to the app's web site.

3. **Menu Location:** For GUI-only apps, this is where to find the app in the Raspbian menu once it's installed. *GUI apps don't have run commands, and command-line apps don't have menu locations*.

4. **Run Command:** For command-line-only apps, this is the command you type to run the app.

5. **Help:** This is the documentation that installs with the app. Most are command-line man pages. Reading man pages is discussed in Chapter 5, but you can try them at any time.

6. **Web Site:** The Internet home page for the app. Software downloads, documentation, and often user forums can be found here.

7. After the heading follow my description, impression, and notes about each app—what's it good for, how easy it is to use, and so forth.

Office Suite—LibreOffice

If you're a heavy user of Microsoft Office, the only feasible replacement in the Raspberry Pi world is LibreOffice. The entire LibreOffice suite comes preinstalled with Raspbian, Ubuntu MATE, and most other distributions as well; so whichever Linux distribution you installed, you probably already have this available. You can find them all under Raspberry ➤ Office.

LibreOffice is an open source workalike for Microsoft Office. There's a full word processor (Writer), spreadsheet (Calc), slideshow maker (Impress), database (Base), drawing app (Draw), and an equation/formula editor (Math). These apps can open and edit documents created in Microsoft Word, Excel, and PowerPoint and offer the most commonly used features of these apps. These apps do not offer 100% of Microsoft's more obscure features, but for most projects, they work just fine.

I'm not a big database or spreadsheet user, but I use the LibreOffice Writer and Impress (Word and PowerPoint clones) quite often, even on the Raspberry Pi. They work reliably and are comfortably fast on the Pi, even with longer documents. Some large apps take a big performance hit by running on the Pi, but I find these apps to be completely frustration-free on the Pi. No sacrifices here.

As you can see in the various screenshots that follow, the menus and interface are very different from their Microsoft counterparts, but all the functionality is there. Everything is well documented, and LibreOffice has an excellent help system that will help you track down any feature that you can't find by browsing the menus.

Now let's look at the different parts of the office suite, one app at a time.

LibreOffice Details:

Installation: `sudo apt install libreoffice` (preinstalled in Raspbian)

Menu location: `Raspberry Menu ➤ Office`

Help: `man libreoffice`

Web site: `www.libreoffice.org/`

LibreOffice Writer

Writer is the word processor included in LibreOffice, comparable to Microsoft Word. I've found that most Microsoft Word documents that don't rely on VBA or macro scripting will load and work just fine in Writer. The files are almost 100% compatible, and only very complex documents will ever have any issues.

Figure 4-1 is an image of this book being worked on in LibreOffice Writer.

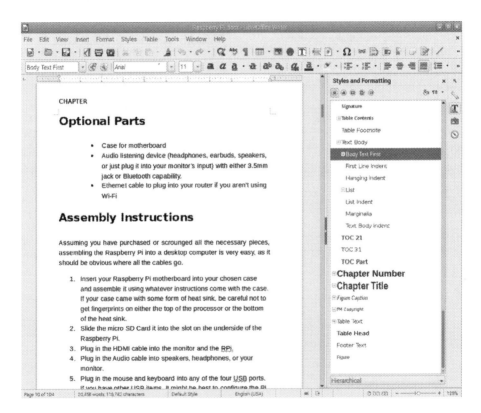

Figure 4-1. *Editing this manuscript in LibreOffice Writer on a Raspberry Pi*

Notice that all the styles are right there in an easy-to-use side pane, just as they would be in Word. Writer also offers features like tracking changes, printing to either a printer or PDF file (among other options), tables, formulas, bibliographies, mail merge, and lots of other advanced features beyond just typing in documents.

LibreOffice Calc

Calc is the spreadsheet portion of LibreOffice, similar in functions to Microsoft Excel. As with Writer, it can save and load Excel files, and with the exception of Excel's macros and VBA script, it can run most spreadsheets without difficulty. It offers relative and absolute referencing, tracking changes, error tracing, pivot tables, and many surprisingly complex calculations. Figure 4-2 is a look at Calc doing some very basic calculations.

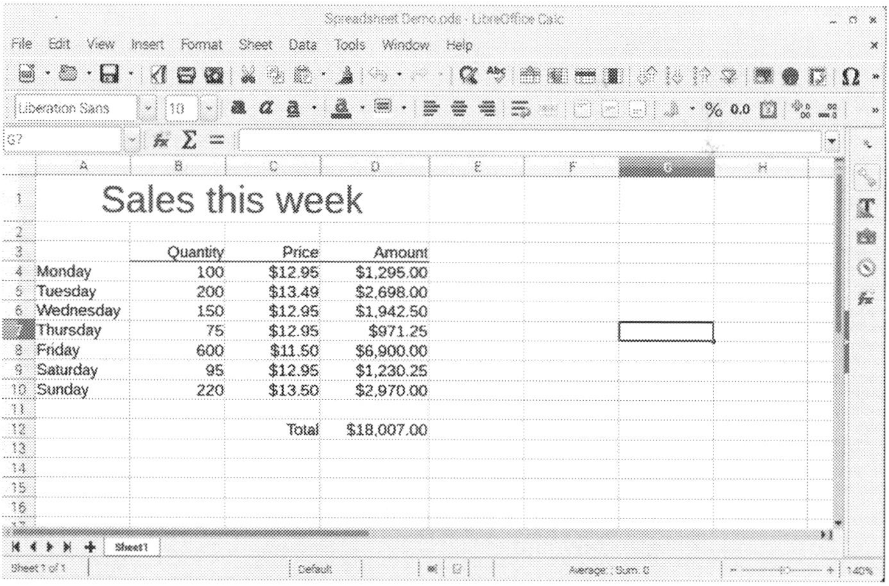

Figure 4-2. *LibreOffice Calc*

LibreOffice Impress

Like the previous two entries, Impress is essentially LibreOffice's feature clone of PowerPoint. Although it doesn't have PowerPoint's impressive collection of themes, it does have nearly all the same features. Figure 4-3 gives us a look at Impress in action.

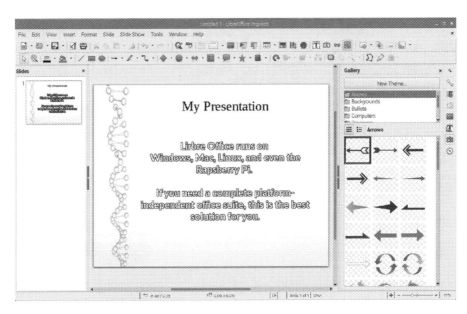

Figure 4-3. *LibreOffice Impress*

Other LibreOffice Tools

The big three apps in LibreOffice are Writer, Calc, and Impress; but there are other apps within the office suite. LibreOffice Draw is a tool for creating flowcharts, diagrams, and any vector-type images. There's also Math, an equation editor for easily creating and formatting mathematical formulas for use in any of the other LibreOffice products. Lastly is Base, a database creation and management app, along the same lines as, but *not* compatible with, Microsoft Access. Most of the databases available for Linux are of the

SQL variety and are designed more for server-side use, so Access doesn't really have any direct clone for us. If this is a major problem, look into Base and then see if there are any other apps that can replicate the specific functionality that you need.

LibreOffice is easily the most powerful choice for an office suite that you can install on the Raspberry Pi, but there are other options available if you can work in the cloud rather than an installed suite.

Microsoft Office

No, Microsoft doesn't make a version of Office, or any other products, for the Raspberry Pi. That said, you can use Microsoft Office Online in your preferred web browser. There are browser-based versions of Word (in Figure 4-4), Excel, and PowerPoint, as well as Outlook and OneNote; and all of them can save and load regular desktop versions of those files. You can find all this at `www.office.com`.

Keep in mind, however, that even though this is a real, official Office product made by Microsoft itself, this cloud version of Office is not even close to feature parity with the desktop version of Microsoft Office. In fact, if you need advanced tools or close compatibility, you are probably better off going with LibreOffice instead of Office Online. On the plus side, the web version is offered by Microsoft for free, and if you only need to do fairly simple work, it is a stable and reliable system that works well. Also, being on the cloud means it can be used anywhere with no need to carry your files around with you.

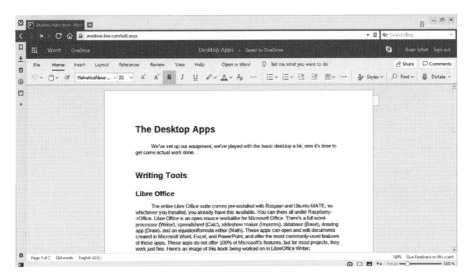

Figure 4-4. *Microsoft Office Online running in the Vivaldi web browser*

Google Docs

Another well-known cloud service is Google Drive or Google Docs (shown in Figure 4-5), and like Microsoft Office, it is a cloud-based service that works well on the Pi. It can be found at `https://drive.google.com`.

All the various parts of Google's office suite (Docs, Sheets, Slides, Drawings, etc.) were designed from the ground up to be a lightweight but powerful "office suite in the cloud," and it's awesome on a regular desktop computer; these are the primary tools for the entire line of Chromebook computers. Google Docs does work reliably on the Pi, but often involves some frustratingly slow page load times. I have found that while it is sometimes uncomfortably laggy in the Chromium browser, it seems to work nicely with the Vivaldi browser. Experiment for yourself and see what works best for you.

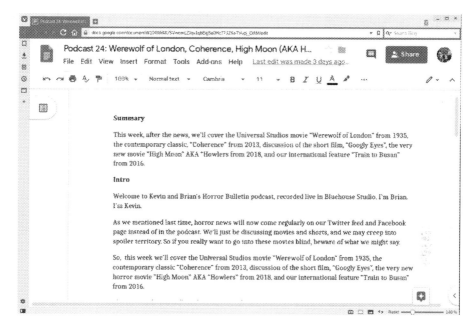

Figure 4-5. *Google Docs running in the Vivaldi browser*

Writing Tools

Most people do some form of writing on their computers. Whether it be notes and papers for school, emails for business, ad copy, programming code, or even the full text of a book, there are tools to help with that. Microsoft Word is the most common "writing solution" on both Windows and Mac, but as you'll soon see, there are many other options in the Linux world.

Scribus

Scribus Details:

Installation: `sudo apt install scribus`

Menu location: `Raspberry Menu ➤ Graphics`

Help: `man scribus`

Web site: `www.scribus.net/`

LibreOffice Writer is the best choice for general word processing, and it can do some page layout functions as well, but for complex page layouts and desktop publishing, there's a better choice: Scribus. Scribus is an open source desktop publisher, similar in function to, but very different from, Microsoft Publisher.

There are numerous monthly magazines produced using Scribus, including the Raspberry Pi Foundation's own *The MagPi Magazine*.

Leafpad (aka Text Editor)

Leafpad Details:

Installation: `sudo apt install leafpad`

Menu location: `Raspberry Menu ➤ Accessories`

Help: `man leafpad`

Web site: `http://tarot.freeshell.org/leafpad/`

Under Raspberry ➤ Accessories is an option simply called "Text Editor." This brings up a bare-bones text editing app known as Leafpad. If you need to edit system files, want to read a file, or simply want to write in plain, mostly unformatted text, this app has you covered. It's really super easy to use, and it compares to WordPad on Windows and TextEdit on Mac.

Note that when you're installing "writing apps," there is a big difference between a word processor and a text editor. A text editor loads and saves pure text, with no special formatting, fonts, or layout options, while a word processor includes formatting such as bold, italic, margins, fonts, colors, and the like. Word processor formats, such as *.docx*, *.odt*, and the like, tie your documents to the specific word processor that created them, while pure text documents, *.txt*, *.md*, or *.tex*, can be read by any text editor.

AbiWord

AbiWord Details:

Installation: `sudo apt install abiword`

Menu location: `Raspberry Menu ➤ Office`

Help: `man abiword`

Web site: `www.abisource.com/`

This word processor doesn't install in Raspbian by default; you'll need to add it. If you don't need all the other apps in the LibreOffice suite and simply want a stand-alone word processor, this is the one to try. It's small and fast, and it's cross-platform, so you can also install it on other computers.

Texmaker

Texmaker Details:

Installation: `sudo apt install texmaker`

Menu location: `Raspberry Menu ➤ Office`

Help: `man texmaker`

Web site: `www.xm1math.net/texmaker/`

This isn't a standard word processor. It's a tool for writing in LaTeX, a text-formatting system we'll discuss more in Chapter 7. To quickly summarize, LaTeX is a text-formatting language that allows you to describe extremely complex and detailed text layouts, equations, math, images, and even things like margins and fonts, all using simple text commands. If this sounds complex, that's because it *is* complex, but tools like Texmaker help ease that complexity significantly. Figure 4-6 shows us an example LaTeX document in the left-hand pane and a compiled, finished document in the right-hand pane.

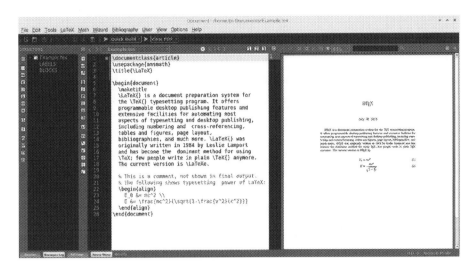

Figure 4-6. *Texmaker specialized LaTeX editor*

PDF Tools

Documents in PDF format are a mainstay of most businesses. How do you create them, and how do you read them on the Pi?

Qpdfview

Qpdfview Details:

Installation: `sudo apt install qpdfview` (preinstalled in Raspbian)

Menu location: `Raspberry Menu ➤ Accessories`

Help: `man qpdfview`

Web site: `https://github.com/bendikro/qpdfview`

If you simply double-click a pdf file in the File Manager, the system will open the file and allow you to view it using an app called *Qpdfview*. It's a simple little app that will let you quickly and easily view pdfs. It doesn't do very much, but it loads quick and is compatible with complex pdf files, so try it out; and if that's all you need, then just stick with that. Why use a complex tool if a simple one will do the job?

Evince

Evince Details:

Installation: `sudo apt install evince`

Menu location: `Raspberry Menu ➤ Office`

Help: `man evince`

Web site: `https://wiki.gnome.org/Apps/Evince`

Evince is the next step-up in PDF readers. You can view two pages side by side, create bookmarks, annotate the text, print, see thumbnails (as in the screenshot in Figure 4-7), and much more. In Figure 4-7, you can see an index of thumbnails on the left and a large, readable page on the right. The views can be configured several different ways, so this is one of the most flexible pdf readers.

Figure 4-7. *Evince PDF reader (an issue of The MagPi is included in Raspbian)*

Okular

Okular Details:

    Installation: `sudo apt install okular`

    Menu location: `Raspberry Menu ➤ Office`

    Help: `man okular`

    Web site: `https://okular.kde.org/`

If you need more advanced tools to work with **and edit** pdfs, then this is the tool you'll want to look at. You can select and edit areas of a document, print, bookmark, reorder pages, and much more. It also does other formats beyond just PDF: Postscript, DjVu, CHM, XPS, EPUB, and others are supported. As you can see in Figure 4-8, Okular has a few more options, but also gives us a more convoluted interface.

Figure 4-8. *Okular PDF manager (The MagPi issue is included free with Raspbian)*

Email

Sending and receiving email is a primary work function for many people. While there's no Outlook or Mail.app on Raspbian, there are some very powerful alternatives.

Thunderbird

Thunderbird Details:

Installation: `sudo apt install thunderbird`
Menu location: `Raspberry Menu ➤ Internet`

Help: `man thunderbird`

Web site: `www.thunderbird.net/`

Thunderbird has been around since 2004, and you can get versions for all the major operating systems. It's comparable in features to Microsoft Outlook, and it's released by Mozilla, the same people who make the Firefox web browser; so they're reliable, established, and not going away anytime soon. If you use a web browser to check your email, that's fine, but if you want an offline mail app, this is the one to try. It includes a contact list, a calendaring app, and lots of other powerful tools.

Configuring your email accounts is usually pretty easy; I put in my Gmail account and password, and it set up everything else for me automatically. The results are shown in Figure 4-9.

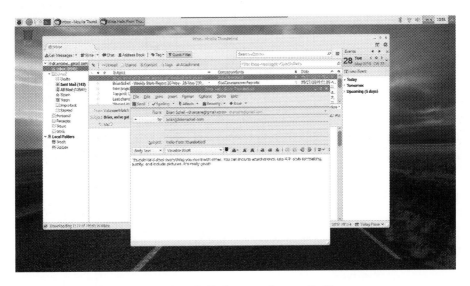

Figure 4-9. *Thunderbird: a full-featured email client*

Claws Mail

Claws Details:

Installation: `sudo apt install claws-mail`

Menu location: `Raspberry Menu ➤ Internet`

Help: `man claws-mail`

Web site: `www.claws-mail.org/`

Claws Mail, shown in Figure 4-10, comes preinstalled in Raspbian, so you already have this available to you. It has several dialogs to help you get your account set up, but it's not as intuitive as Thunderbird; you may need to check out the instructions your web provider offers in order to configure POP3, SMTP, and IMAP settings manually. It's also nowhere near as full featured as Thunderbird, but, once it's configured, it's simple and really fast to use on the Pi, so this may be all you need.

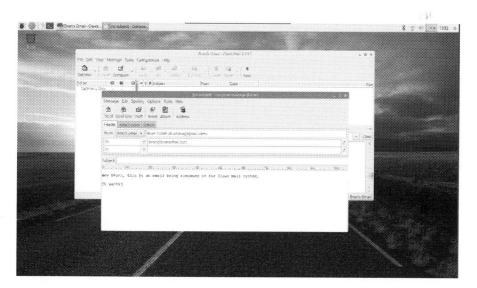

Figure 4-10. *Claws Mail client*

Web Browsers

Many of us spend most of our computer time sitting in front of a web browser. Anything anyone could ever want to know is out there on the Web, somewhere, and the tool you use to access that information is important.

If you love Chrome on your Windows or Mac, you'll still want to use it here; but other options, like Vivaldi, Firefox, and Tor, are also available. We'll take a look at the differences between them now.

Chromium

Chromium Details:

Installation: `sudo apt install chromium` (preinstalled in Raspbian)

Menu location: `Raspberry Menu ➤ Internet`

Help: `man chromium`

Web site: `www.chromium.org/`

Chromium is the browser that's included in Raspbian, and it's the open source version of Google's Chrome browser. A lot of the code that is embedded in Chromium eventually makes it into regular Chrome.

You can log in to Google using your Google account (this is the same as your Gmail account if you have one), and all your bookmarks, menu settings, themes, extensions, and everything else will sync over quickly, giving you an experience just like any other version of Chrome. For most web sites and situations, this is the fastest browser for use with Raspbian, although some other browsers may have the edge if you are using a different distribution. I'd recommend trying several different browsers and then picking whichever one works the best for your working style.

Firefox

Firefox Details:

Installation: `sudo apt install firefox`

Menu location: `Raspberry Menu ➤ Internet`

Help: `man firefox`

Web site: `www.mozilla.org/en-US/firefox/new/`

Many businesses and groups have standardized their office on Firefox, since Mozilla places a much higher value on user's privacy than Google.

If you are used to using Firefox elsewhere, then it's easy to install and use it on your Pi as well—once you log in with your Firefox account and password, all your bookmarks and settings should import from the cloud, so the experience should be just like using Firefox on any other computer.

Then follow the onscreen instructions to log in and sync your bookmarks if you want, or just start browsing. Note that as of the time of this writing, the version of Firefox available for the Pi is version 52.9, which is **2 years old**; Mozilla is not currently developing updates for the Raspberry Pi, so as time continues to pass, this will fall further and further out of date, which may cause security issues. That being said, Firefox *does* currently work, and it works well. There's no way to be sure if they will update it or continue to release new updates.

Vivaldi

Vivaldi Details:

Installation: (see in the following)

Menu location: Raspberry Menu ➤ Internet

Help: (see web site)

Web site: http://vivaldi.com

Vivaldi is a newer browser that has lots of fun new features. It's extremely customizable, allowing you to put tabs in stacks and groups, split the browser window in various ways, and even put a notes app within the browser itself. I have found that on the Pi, it's often significantly faster loading pages than Chromium. It's worth a few minutes of your time to check out the introductory video on their web site, http://vivaldi.com.

It's a little more involved to install, since it's not included in Raspbian, nor is it in the "apt" repositories. Type the following one line at a time:

```
sudo apt update
```

```
sudo apt upgrade
```

```
wget https://downloads.vivaldi.com/stable/vivaldi-
stable_1.13.1008.34-1_armhf.deb
```

```
sudo apt install ./vivaldi-stable_1.13.1008.34-1_armhf.deb
```

This is interesting to note because this is the process you would generally use to install any "Debian package" that is not specifically included in the Raspbian repositories. The first two lines simply update the repository information on your Pi and also update any software that needs updating. The third line (*wget*) downloads the installation file, and the fourth line installs the app using the familiar "*sudo apt install*" process. You would need to know the exact URL for the .deb file, so this isn't something you can just work out for yourself, but you might find an install of this kind as you find apps on the Web that aren't available in the built-in repositories.

The Tor Browser

Tor Details:

Installation: `sudo apt install tor`

Run command: `tor`

Help: `man tor`

Web site: `www.torproject.org/`

Tor is a system for combining a VPN (Virtual Private Network) and a web browser. It's a browser that will disguise your location and any trackable information about you. For truly private browsing, this is a tool to look into.

On Windows and Mac, you can simply download the Tor Browser and use it as you would any other browser. The Tor Browser is not available on the Raspberry Pi, but there is a workaround. You can install the server version of Tor and then make the Chromium browser work through it.

This makes your web activity very hard to trace. Once Tor is installed, just go to the command line and type

```
chromium-browser --proxy-server=socks5://localhost:9050
```

This will run the Chromium browser that's already installed and make all output go through Tor's VPN-like system. When I ran the preceding command, I then went to Google Maps, shown in Figure 4-11, to see where it *thought* I was located. It showed me a location in Kharkiv, Ukraine!

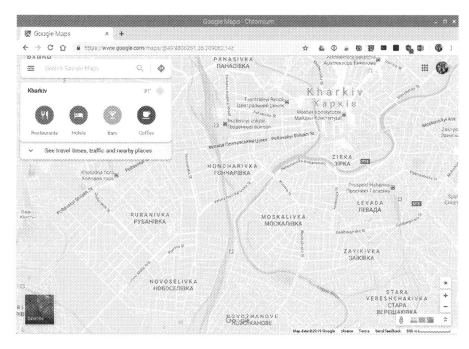

Figure 4-11. *I am NOT in Ukraine, but it looks that way to the rest of the Internet!*

Notes Apps

There are no apps specifically included with Raspbian that cater to notes and saving information installed in Raspbian. You could use the Leafpad text editor or LibreOffice Writer discussed previously, but those are often overkill for a simple list or note.

GNote

GNote Details:

    Installation: `sudo apt install gnote`

    Menu location: `Raspberry Menu ➤ Accessories`

    Help: `man gnote`

    Web site: `https://wiki.gnome.org/Apps/Gnote`

    This is a super-simple notebook app that easily lets you type or cut and paste text into a note and even allows you to link notes together. Although you can do basic formatting like bold, italic, and underlining, there is no way to insert images or other non-text items. The goal with GNote is to be as simple as possible. When you run it, you will see something like Figure 4-12.

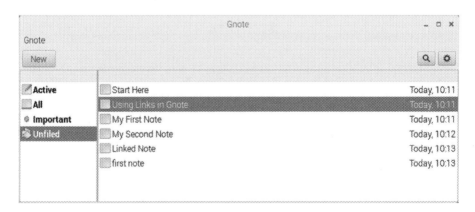

Figure 4-12. *GNote with a couple quick notes added*

OneNote

OneNote is part of the Microsoft Office suite, and like Word and Excel, it also has an online component. It's one of the most powerful note-taking apps available, whether on the Pi or elsewhere; and everything you enter into it syncs to your iPhone, Android, or other computers seamlessly. You have multiple ways of organizing your data—individual notebooks, or sections within those notebooks, and then on individual pages. There's a lot of flexibility; and you can include text, images, pdfs, and even sound files. Unlike the other Office apps, OneNote is free to use on all platforms for everyone.

Figure 4-13 shows my color-coded sections on the left, the names of a couple of pages in the middle column, and a clipped article in the main pane.

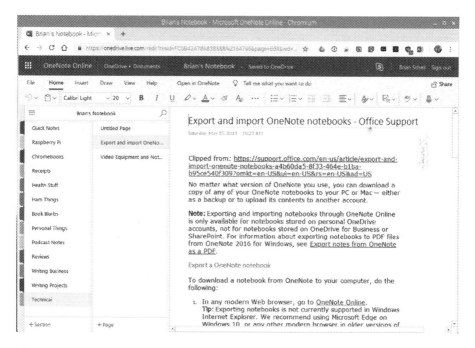

Figure 4-13. *Microsoft OneNote running in Chromium*

You can learn more about OneNote at `www.onenote.com`.

Zim

Zim Details:

Installation: `sudo apt install zim`

Menu location: `Raspberry Menu ➤ Accessories`

Help: `man zim`

Web site: `https://zim-wiki.org/`

Zim (Figure 4-14) is a desktop *wiki*. A wiki is a method of collecting, linking, and organizing a bunch of pages of data. If you're familiar with Wikipedia, you have the idea, but this is much simpler and easier to manage. All data is stored in plain text files with wiki formatting. If you usually just enter a bunch of random things in your notebooks, this app may be overkill; but if your notes require any kind of organization, whether simple or complex, this is worth checking out. It also allows storage of text, links, photos, task lists, and equation editor and accepts plug-ins for expansion.

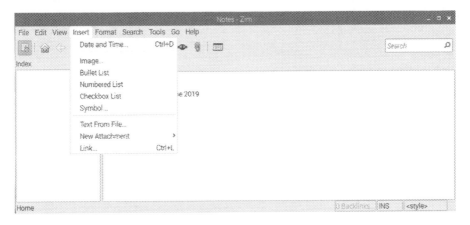

Figure 4-14. Zim desktop wiki

Zim is available for Windows, Mac, Linux, and many other platforms; so if syncing your data is important, Zim has you covered. You can learn more about Zim at `https://zim-wiki.org`.

Cherrytree

Cherrytree Details:

    Installation: (see in the following)

    Menu location: Raspberry Menu ➤ Accessories

    Help: man cherrytree

    Web site: www.giuspen.com/cherrytree/

Cherrytree is another wiki, similar in many ways to Zim, but it's far more complex and allows a vast number of customizations and features. It's got a much more modern interface than Zim. It can store text, images, files, links, tables, and executable snippets of code. It allows you to contain all your data in a single xml file, or if you have a huge number of notes, you can store them in an SQL database. Cherrytree is available for Linux and Windows, but there is no Mac version, so keep that in mind if you are considering syncing your data between machines.

To install, go to a command line and carefully type the following two lines:

```
wget http://www.giuspen.com/software/cherrytree_0.38.8-0_all.deb
sudo apt install ./cherrytree_0.38.8-0_all.deb
```

Figure 4-15 shows the Raspberry Pi edition.

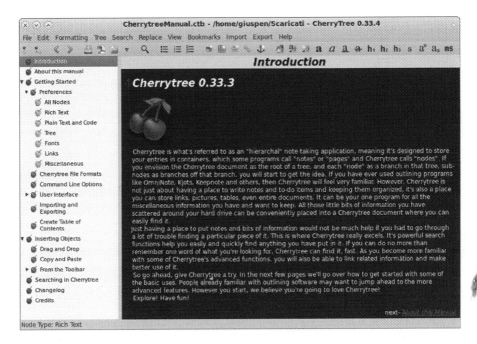

Figure 4-15. *Cherrytree—a powerful wiki with many options*

Audio, Video, and Graphics Editing

Audio and video editing are notoriously processor-intensive tasks, and many companies sell incredibly expensive graphic workstations for video work. Video rendering is one of the primary uses of Apple's new $6000 Mac Pro computers. Can a Raspberry Pi compete with *that?*

Well, no. Still, audio editing with Audacity is fully possible, and it works quite well. In addition, the Raspberry Pi model 4 can load in, convert, save, and do some simple edits to your videos using Kdenlive.

Older models of the RPi … Well, you can try, but the experience is really not very good; the older Pi models just do not have the RAM required to load in large audio and video files. That said, the apps do run, even on the older models, and do work; so if these are tools that you need, then enjoy!

Audacity

Audacity Details:

Installation: `sudo apt install audacity`

Menu location: `Raspberry Menu ➤ Sound & Video`

Help: `man audacity`

Web site: `https://sourceforge.net/projects/audacity/`

On "regular" computers, Audacity is known far and wide for being the most feature-packed open source sound editing system. It has plug-ins, effects, macros, and a ton of other features. I personally have edited everything from podcasts to audiobooks using Audacity on my Mac.

Audacity for the Raspberry Pi, as shown in Figure 4-16, has most of the same features found on a full-powered computer, which is good, but it's painfully slow to do very much with it on anything less than the model 4 Pi. The problem is not the app itself, but the size of the sound files, which often get quite large; the Pi model 3B+ and older models just don't have enough RAM to work with those files efficiently. Still, for things like saving a file in a different format or doing little edits, it works fine on the older Pi!

That said, with the new Raspberry Pi 4, it works without trouble. Really large files may still run into limitations due to RAM, but most short recordings can be loaded and edited just fine.

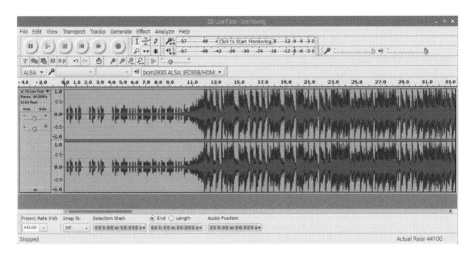

Figure 4-16. *Audacity sound editor on the Raspberry Pi*

Kdenlive

Kdenlive Details:

Installation: (see in the following)

Menu location: Raspberry Menu ➤ Sound & Video

Help: man kdenlive

Web site: https://kdenlive.org/en/

Whereas Audacity works with sound files, Kdenlive works with video. Where Audacity works quite well on the Pi model 4, Kdenlive still somewhat struggles with video. It runs, it loads files, but in all honesty, video editing is really not something even the newest Pi is going to be good at, simply because video files are **huge**. Still, it installs and runs, so play around with it if you're curious.

Install with

```
sudo apt install breeze-icon-theme
sudo apt install kdenlive
```

VLC Player

VLC Player Details:

Installation: `sudo apt install vlc`

Menu location: `Raspberry Menu ➤ Sound & Video`

Help: `man vlc`

Web site: `www.videolan.org/vlc/index.html`

Editing video is a little much for the Raspberry Pi, but watching them is a whole lot easier. If you just want to watch videos, you cannot go wrong with VLC Player, shown in Figure 4-17. It includes many of the video codecs you need to play various video and music formats and lets you play either movies or music playlists, use subtitles, and do streaming; and it's very configurable to boot.

The model 3B+ RPi cannot deal with 4K videos, but for 720p and even most 1080p videos, it works just fine. With the model 4 Pi, video output was one of the primary goals of the upgrade. Not only can it easily handle 4K video but it can do it with two monitors at once. Video performance was one of the main goals for the upgrade, so you can truly say that it's *built* for video output with two 4K HDMI outputs.

Figure 4-17. *Watching a video with VLC Player*

Music Players

Once in a while, it's fun to listen to music. VLC, mentioned earlier, will play music and playlists just great, but an app that specializes in music management and library-keeping is going to offer a lot more features. I have known people who have taken a dedicated Raspberry Pi and included them in various types of jukebox and antique radio lookalike projects. We're not going to go that far here, but here are a trio of great MP3 players that you can try. In addition to regular music files, if you're into audio podcasts, both Amarok and Clementine both work with them easily.

Amarok Details:

Installation: `sudo apt install amarok`

Menu location: `Raspberry Menu ➤ Sound & Video`

Help: `man amarok`

Web site: `https://amarok.kde.org/`

Amarok is a player that can handle all the audio files stored on your computer and can handle a large number of streaming web services as well. Last.fm, LibriVox, MP3Tunes, podcasts, and many more sites and services are supported.

Qmmp Details:

Installation: `sudo apt install qmmp`

Menu location: `Raspberry Menu ➤ Sound & Video`

Help: `man qmmp`

Web site: `http://qmmp.ylsoftware.com/`

Qmmp for many years, the go-to music player on Windows, was an app called Winamp. The developer gave up on updating and developing Winamp several years ago, but this Winamp-lookalike app is available and works very well. It handles MP3 files and playlists and does it all in style. If you remember Winamp, take a look at Qmmp.

Clementine Details:

Installation: `sudo apt install clementine`

Menu location: `Raspberry Menu ➤ Sound & Video`

Help: `man clementine`

Web site: `www.clementine-player.org/`

Clementine is cross-platform, so if you create bunch of playlists on your Pi, you can move them elsewhere without issues. It's similar in many ways to iTunes in that it does just about everything. Clementine will manage your library, connect to web services, and a host of other functions. Figure 4-18 shows the RPi version.

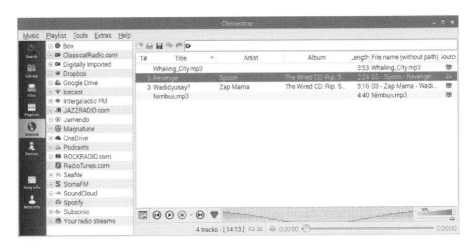

Figure 4-18.   *Clementine music player showing off its array of web services*

GIMP

GIMP Details:

Installation: `sudo apt install gimp`

Menu Location: `Raspberry Menu ➤ Graphics`

Help: `man gimp`

Web site: `www.gimp.org/`

GIMP, shown in Figure 4-19, is short for the GNU Image Manipulation Program and is a very feature-packed graphic editor, in the same class as Adobe's Photoshop. Unlike the audio and video editors we discussed a few pages ago, GIMP works just fine on the Pi. Some of the image calculations and complicated renders may be slow at times, but it's not too bad, and there are no slowdowns in actually working with the app; it's not at all painful.

There are built-in "scripts" that make logos, buttons, and other net things, there are many filters and editing settings, and they all work on the Pi. It's an extremely capable and complex app, able to do nearly anything with an image, but all this power comes with a steep learning curve. Fortunately, it's a popular app, and there are many books and videos available to show you how to get started.

As usual, this can be installed with `sudo apt install gimp`.

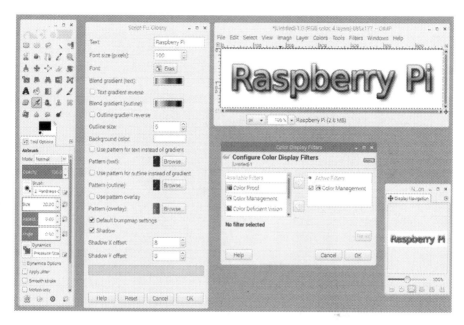

Figure 4-19. *GIMP: GNU Image Manipulation Program*

Inkscape

Inkscape Details:

Installation: `sudo apt install inkscape`

Menu location: `Raspberry Menu ➤ Graphics`

Help: `man inkscape`

Web site: `https://inkscape.org/`

GIMP is awesome and very powerful for editing photos and creating photo-like images. On the opposite side of the coin are vector graphics, where designs are made by recording a series of points and then "connecting the dots," making these images infinitely scalable, which is useful for logos, posters, and visual designs where the size can change. The app that's best for this on the Pi is Inkscape. Inkscape is roughly equivalent to Adobe Illustrator, where GIMP is more comparable to Adobe Photoshop—different tools for different jobs! Figure 4-20 shows us a zoomed-in Father's Day image.

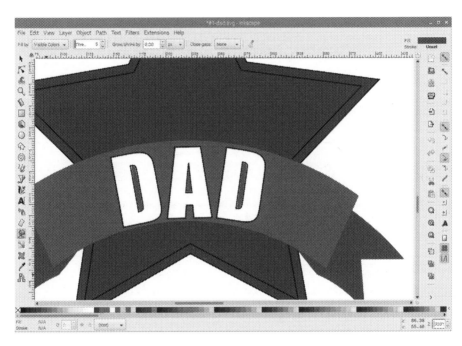

Figure 4-20. *Vector SVG file loaded into Inkscape on the Pi*

File Management Apps

Much of the file management on the Pi is handled through the File Manager app or even through a text-based file app like Midnight Commander (see Chapter 5) or even Linux command-line file manipulation tools like mv and cp (we'll see these later). Still, sometimes you need more complicated ways of moving files around, and this is often far more easily done using a visual tool from the desktop.

FileZilla

FileZilla Details:

Installation: `sudo apt install filezilla`

Menu location: `Raspberry Menu ➤ Internet`

Help: `man filezilla`

Web site: `https://filezilla-project.org/`

Created by the Mozilla Foundation, the same people who made Firefox and Thunderbird, FileZilla is a safe and powerful FTP manager. You can keep a list of FTP servers, complete with login information on hand, and transfer files between them easily. Need to copy a bunch of music files from your PC? This is one way to do it.

You can browse through all your files on the Pi in the left-hand pane and all the remote files and directories on the remote machine in the right-hand pane and then just copy, move, delete, or whatever you want to do, easily, using the mouse.

FileZilla uses either plain ftp or sftp for added security. If your file transfers get interrupted, they are easily resumed, continuing where the first batch failed. This is my favorite way to get files into and out of my Pi at home from another computer on the same network. You can see me connecting to my Mac in Figure 4-21; the local RPi files are on the left, and the files on the right are in my Mac's hard drive. Just drag and drop to move files from one to the other, and it's just as easy to move whole folders.

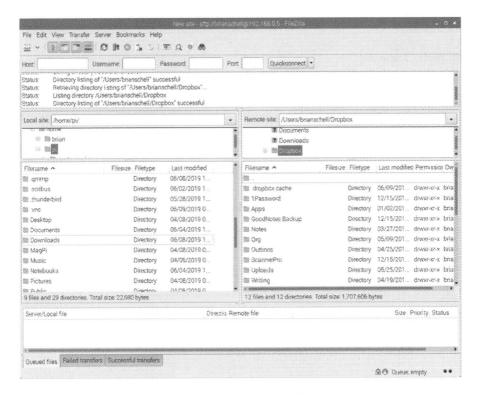

Figure 4-21. *Accessing my Mac from FileZilla running on the Pi*

Deluge

Deluge Details:

Installation: `sudo apt install deluge`

Menu location: `Raspberry Menu ➤ Internet`

Help: `man deluge`

Web site: `https://deluge-torrent.org/`

Deluge is a cross-platform BitTorrent client, and there's a screenshot in Figure 4-22. BitTorrent has always been a little controversial, as it's often used as a way to pirate movies and music, but it has a lot of legitimate uses as well. Most, if not all, distributions of Linux can be downloaded through a BitTorrent system, and the files usually transfer faster than a plain download. Whatever your purpose in running a torrent, Deluge is the solution for doing it on the Pi. Go to a site that offers *.torrent* files and download it somewhere on your Pi. Load up Deluge and open up the .torrent file with it, and the target file will download.

Figure 4-22. *Downloading BitTorrent via Deluge app*

Conclusion

We've discussed a large number of apps now, and these are, at least in my opinion, the best apps for these particular jobs. There *are* other apps that do the same things that I haven't mentioned, and if you aren't happy with some of my suggestions, then there are probably alternatives available with a quick online search. Even more likely is that there is some task you need to do that I haven't even thought of. If this is the case, then go through the Raspbian software installer we talked about in the previous chapter and see if there is an easy-to-install tool that does what you need.

If not, you can do a Google search to see if someone has already solved the problem in some way. All these apps are open source solutions, and most open source developers are eager to solve problems and suggest tools.

We've looked at the desktop GUI interface in the previous chapter and the apps in this chapter. Now, we'll do the same things for the command-line interface: first the interface tools and then the apps. Hang on, the choices explode from here!

CHAPTER 5

Using the Command-Line Tools

Over the past two decades, we've all gotten used to using GUI apps and desktops, but before that, everything was done in text mode on terminal screens. If you remember the days of MS-DOS or UNIX, then you know the drill. It was all command line, all the time. And somehow, we still managed to get our work done.

The simple fact is that in many ways, sticking with only the command line is often *much* faster and more efficient. For example, to save a file in the GUI, you need to reach over to the mouse, move the mouse to the *File* menu, click the *Save* command, then move your hand back to the keyboard and resume typing. That's a lot of moving and interaction. Or you could hit Ctrl-S on the keyboard instead. It's a trade-off. It's faster using the keyboard, but you have to spend the time to *learn* it. Repeating this time savings hundreds of times a day really can add up to more time available for other things.

Many text-based apps don't rely on, or even support, the mouse. Keyboard commands are usually considered "power user tricks" today, but without the mouse, they become a necessity. Productivity skyrockets when you can keep both hands on the keyboard at all times.

© Brian Schell 2019
B. Schell, *Computing with the Raspberry Pi*, https://doi.org/10.1007/978-1-4842-5293-2_5

Of course, if you are into desktop publishing or video editing, then you really do need graphical tools. Some things just need the GUI. On the other hand, there are many, *many* tasks that can be done just as well, if not more efficiently, using only the keyboard. If you thought using the Raspberry Pi as your only computer was a fun challenge, try doing it all in text mode!

In this chapter, we'll look at some of the basic tools that are used to get things done in text mode. This is not a comprehensive tutorial on Linux commands, but we do look at some of the commands, as well as tools you can use along with or sometimes instead of those commands. We'll first look at Tmux, an app that lets you control multiple "windows" of text at once; then we'll look at a better terminal app than the one included in Raspbian; and finally, we will look at two file managers that will make your experience moving, copying, backing up, and deleting files *much* easier. Last, we'll review some of the basic Linux/Unix file commands that let you manually copy files, move them, delete them, and so forth.

Spicing Up the Command Line

You probably picture the command line as a black screen with a few lines of complex and obscure green text on it. And if that's what you want, you can certainly do it that way, but there are numerous tools that make staying in the text mode much more like running a windowing GUI. The app Tmux gives you multiple windows. Terminator gives you nice color schemes, font choices, and a different way to split up your screen. Midnight Commander and Ranger make file operations easier and more powerful than trying to memorize a bunch of commands. We'll look at all these and spice up that boring command line!

Tmux

Tmux Details:

Installation: `sudo apt install tmux`

Run command: `tmux`

Dotfile: `~/.tmux.conf`

Help: `man tmux`

Web site: `https://github.com/tmux/tmux`

With a GUI like Windows or MacOS, or even Raspbian's desktop, when you want to run more than one app at a time, you simply run each app in its own little window. You can position these windows next to each other, overlap them if you want, or minimize them completely. With text-mode terminal apps, you only have one screen, so you need to split that screen up into sections and run one app in each section. Effectively, you get the same result, but it requires a little more planning in advance. Figure 5-1 shows two apps running in a single window using an app called Tmux.

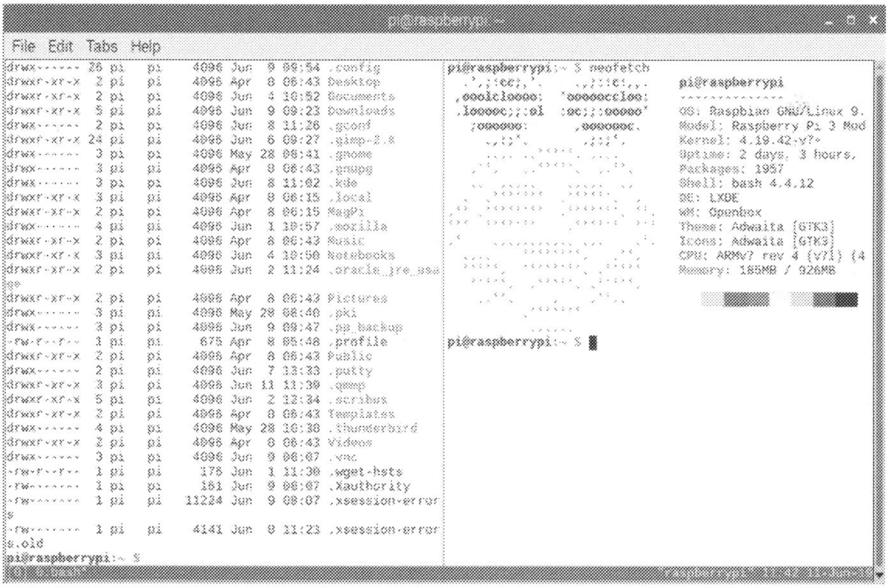

Figure 5-1. *Tmux in use*

Tmux is what is known as a "terminal multiplexer." That's a fancy way of saying it splits your terminal window into smaller panes that each can run a separate program. Figure 5-1 shows a single terminal window running two apps: Vim on the left and a directory listing on the right. This is all done through Tmux.

It doesn't look like much; probably all you will notice is a colored bar at the bottom of the window. This is typical of command-line apps; they often don't have fancy menus.

You control Tmux by pressing the Tmux "command key," which by default is **Ctrl-B**. To make something happen, you press Ctrl-B and some other key depending on what you want to do. For example, to split the screen vertically, as in Figure 5-1, press Ctrl-B and then press %. Note that to get to %, you also have to hold down the Shift key, so that really works out to be Ctrl-B and then Shift-5 (to get % on a US keyboard).

Table 5-1 provides a quick list of the most commonly used Tmux commands. You can split the screen into multiple *panes*, and/or you can have multiple *windows*, which are whole screens.

Table 5-1. *Various Tmux Commands*

Action	Key Combination
Split window vertically	Ctrl-b %
Split window horizontally	Ctrl-b "
New window	Ctrl-b c
Close window	Ctrl-d OR Ctrl-b x
Kill window	Ctrl-b &
Next window	Ctrl-b n
Previous window	Ctrl-b p
Rename window	Ctrl-b ,
List all windows	Ctrl-b w

(*continued*)

Table 5-1. (*continued*)

Action	Key Combination
Move to window number	Ctrl-b [number]
Next pane	Ctrl-b o
Previous pane	Ctrl-b ;
Show pane numbers	Ctrl-b q
Move pane left	Ctrl-b {
Move pane right	Ctrl-b }
Swap pane locations	Ctrl-b Ctrl-o
Resize pane down	Ctrl-b Ctrl-j
Resize pane up	Ctrl-b Ctrl-k
Resize pane left	Ctrl-b Ctrl-h
Resize pane right	Ctrl-b Ctrl-l

That *looks* like a lot to remember, but you'll catch on to them quickly enough with use. In the beginning, all you need to remember is Ctrl-B and then either % or " to split the window either vertically or horizontally; then use Ctrl-B and the arrow keys to navigate between the panes.

In Chapter 7, I will walk you through my "dotfile" configuration file for Tmux, showing you one easy way to change any of these key bindings and otherwise change Tmux's behavior.

It's good to get into the habit of opening the terminal app of your choice and then loading Tmux immediately before anything else. That way, if you find yourself needing another app, you can just pop open another window and have it right there. Of course, you can still open two or three or fifteen different terminal windows if you prefer, but again, by staying inside Tmux, you aren't slowing yourself down with the mouse.

Note If you are booting into text mode (with no GUI at all), then Tmux is the only way you can have more than one app running at a time.

Terminator

Terminator Details:

Installation: `sudo apt install terminator`

Run command: `tmux`

Dotfile: `~/.tmux.conf`

Help: `man terminator`

Web site: `https://gnometerminator.blogspot.com/`

While the previous app, Tmux, runs in a general terminal window and splits up what you see in different ways, Terminator is an app that replaces the built-in terminal app itself and runs multiple resizable terminal panels in one window.

Terminator isn't a text-based app exactly; it's a replacement for the Linux terminal. If you like the regular terminal app that comes with Raspbian, or if you'd prefer to stick with the more commonly used Tmux method of splitting screens, you can skip this one. On the other hand, I like the customizations of colors and fonts, and I think it just *looks* nicer, as you can see in Figure 5-2.

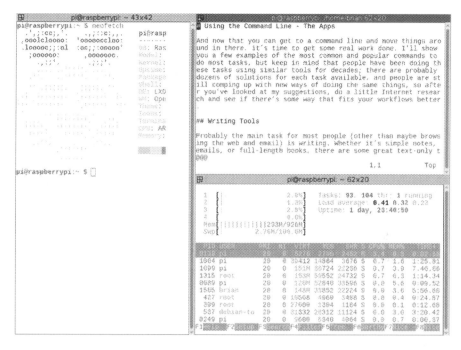

Figure 5-2. *A trio of Terminator panes*

Ranger and Midnight Commander

Ranger Details:

Installation: `sudo apt install ranger`

Run command: `ranger`

Dotfile: various files inside `~/.config/ranger/`

Help: `man ranger`

Web site: `https://github.com/ranger/rangera`

Midnight Commander Details:

Installation: `sudo apt install mc`

Run command: `mc`

Dotfile: various files inside `/etc/mc/`

Help: `man mc`

Web site: `https://midnight-commander.org`

Both Midnight Commander and Ranger are file managers. They allow you to easily navigate your computer's folder hierarchy and copy, move, rename, and delete files, as well as look at previews of the file contents.

It's completely possible to ignore these two and simply copy files with Unix commands like *cp, mv, rm, ls*, and so forth; and sometimes it *is* faster to simply type out your commands. Still, it's definitely a wise move to learn all the Unix file manipulation commands so you *can* do things quickly. If you like purely working at a command-line shell, like the one in Figure 5-3, you are always free to do so.

Sometimes, on the other hand, you want to do things with batches of files or more visually browse and navigate your files. Both Midnight Commander and Ranger are good in their own ways, but it's probably most efficient to pick one or the other and learn to get really good with it.

Ranger has a more "open" feel to it, with two levels of directory in the leftmost two panes and a file preview in the third pane. Movement is fast and highly visual, but there aren't any controls or menus onscreen—it's *all* done through memorized keyboard commands, which slows you down in the beginning. As Figure 5-4 shows, it's very clean and sparse in what it shows.

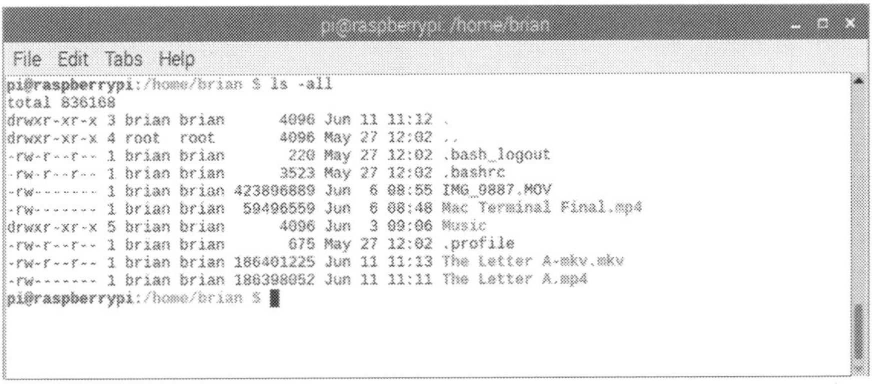

Figure 5-3. File listing on the plain command line

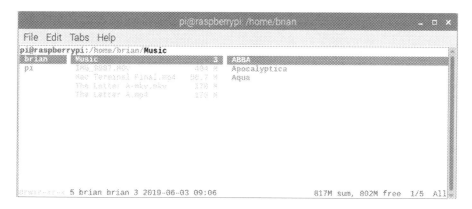

Figure 5-4. *File listing with Ranger*

Midnight Commander, on the other hand, offers a permanent two-column view as shown in Figure 5-5. This is nice for copying files or comparing folders, and there's even a built-in file editing system. There are also menus at the top of the screen, which are easily navigable by either the keyboard or (gasp!) the mouse.

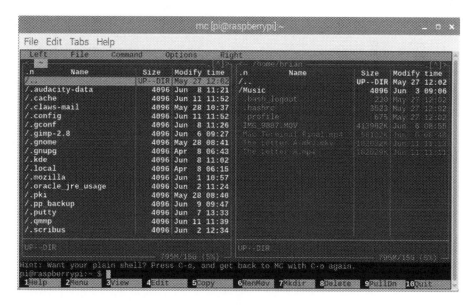

Figure 5-5. *File listing with Midnight Commander*

Which one you use is entirely up to you. They both do exactly the same things, but their interfaces are completely different. I generally do most file-moving command things right on the command line—see the next section for more on that. If I want to quickly move to a song or load a text file, I'll zoom quickly to it in Ranger. When I'm doing something with deeply nested paths, or on the occasion where I don't know where something is or need to dig through a bunch of files and directories, I'll use Midnight Commander.

Using the Raspberry Pi As a Terminal

So far in this book, we've spent lots of time talking about command-line apps and tools that you can run in a terminal window locally on your Pi computer. We've even talked about setting your Pi up to run "headless" with no monitor or keyboard. With a headless setup like this, you access the Pi from some other computer using SSH or VNC Viewer.

Those very same tools will work on large remote computers as well, so if you ever come across some application or process that your RPi really, truly, just cannot handle, you may want to look into running that process on someone else's computer. You can "rent" a remote server from companies such as Linode.com and DigitalOcean.com for two common examples. These systems are inexpensive, at around $5 a month to start, and they are infinitely scalable.

You can sit at your Raspberry Pi, monitor, and mouse and use SSH and VNC Viewer in the terminal app of your choice to work on remote servers. Back in the early chapters, we looked at the built-in Ubuntu Terminal as well as Terminator, but there are literally dozens of other choices here that you can run from the desktop or full-screen command line. You can even access Mac or Windows PCs in this manner, assuming you have them set up with the proper remote access software. If you can't solve all your problems with a Pi, perhaps you can use it as a window to a larger machine that can do what you need.

Back in the 1970s–1980s, this kind of client-server pairing was very common. People would use "dumb" terminals to connect to "smart" computers and mainframes to get work done. In the age of personal computers, that way of thinking went away for a few decades. Now, in the modern age of "everything is connected to the Internet," it's nothing unusual to do work "in the cloud."

With this style of work, you don't need much more than a good terminal program like Terminator, which we'll discuss later, and VNC Viewer, which comes preinstalled with Raspbian. All the computing power you need resides out in the cloud, and your Pi system is more than enough to do literally *anything* this way.

SSH

SSH Details:

Installation: `sudo apt install ssh`

Run command: `ssh <hostname>`

Dotfile: `~/.ssh/config and /etc/ssh/ssh_config`

Help: `man ssh`

Web site: `www.openssh.com/`

The SSH app allows you to log in (via text mode) from your terminal screen to another computer's text-only terminal. Anything you can do in your Raspberry Pi terminal, you can do remotely on another computer as well. If you need more disk space or Internet bandwidth than you can manage at home, you can "rent" computer time at a server farm and "remote in" from your Pi. Figure 5-6 shows my Mac running Midnight Commander, but I'm actually sitting in front of my Pi, while my Mac is in a room upstairs.

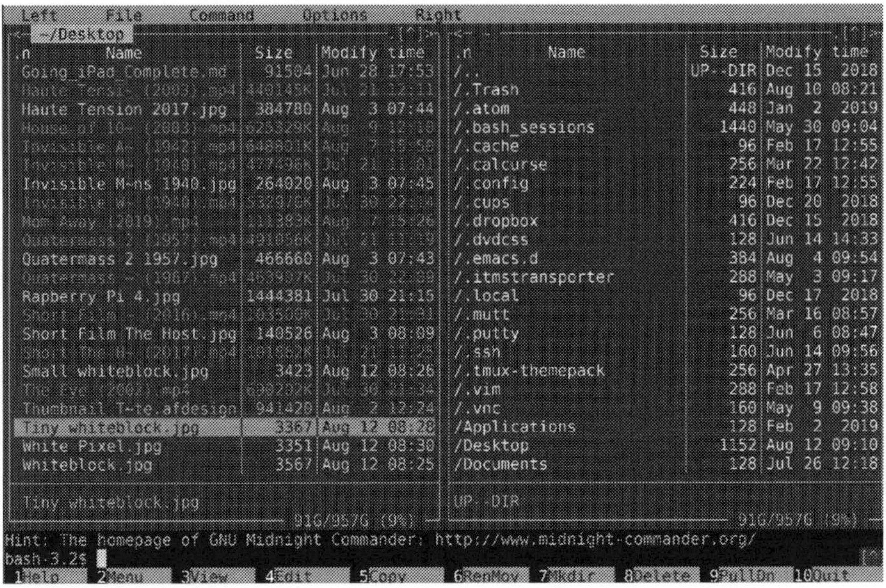

Figure 5-6. *Accessing my Mac via SSH on the Raspberry Pi*

VNC Viewer

VNC Viewer Details:

Installation: (see web site)

Menu location: Raspberry Menu ➤ Internet

Help: man vncviewer

Web site: www.realvnc.com/en/connect/download/viewer/
raspberrypi/

We discussed setting up the Raspberry Pi as a VNC server back in
Chapter 3, and this app does just the opposite; it is the tool you use to log
into a computer running the VNC server. It's like having a complete remote
desktop: you can sit in your office and your monitor shows you the desktop
of a computer potentially thousands of miles away that you control with
your keyboard and mouse.

Figure 5-7 shows my Mac desktop being accessed from my Raspberry
Pi desktop computer. Yes, I can really actually run my Mac apps from my

Pi desktop; some things are a little slower than they would be natively, but they do work. And the VNC software is FREE on both the Pi and the Mac (and PC as well). This is a super-powerful tool that doesn't cost a cent.

Figure 5-7. *My Mac via VNC Viewer*

Essential Linux Commands

For the most part, 90% of what you'll enter on the command line are the names of apps. We'll look at many of them in the next chapter. Emacs, Calcurse, Vim, and even more utility-style apps such as apt and shutdown are really just little programs of their own. Sometimes you need to manipulate a file or a directory, and that's where this section comes in. Note that all of these commands and much more can be done through an interface such as Midnight Commander, so even when living on the command line, some of these are optional. Still, sometimes it's just faster or more convenient to simply type in commands rather than work with menus.

Clearing the Screen

One of the simplest and most often-used commands in my experience is simply that of cleaning up the messy screen. If you want to clear off the screen, just type

```
clear
```

at the command line. You'll see a refreshed, uncluttered terminal screen. It doesn't do much, but over the years, I've probably typed this command more than anything else.

Quitting the Terminal

If you're running a terminal window, you can simply type exit to end your session and close the window. If you used the option to boot into full-screen mode, then you can't just exit the terminal; you'll need to use the reboot or shutdown commands instead.

Listing Files with ls

ls is short for either "list" or "list structure." By itself, it simply lists all the files in the current directory.

```
ls gives the output

Desktop     Downloads    MagPi       Music       'Podsafe Music'
Templates
Documents   Dropbox      Main.org    Pictures    Public
Videos
```

By adding some parameters and options, you can do a lot more:

-l shows the list in the long format, displaying Linux file types, permissions, number of hard links, owner, group, size, last-modified date, and filename.

-a lists all files in the given directory, including those whose names start with "." (which are hidden files in Unix). By default, these files are excluded from the list.

-R recursively lists subdirectories. For example, the command ls -R / would list all files on the system.

-d shows information about a symbolic link or directory, rather than about the link's target or listing the contents of a directory.

-t sorts the list of files by modification time.

-h prints sizes in human-readable format (e.g., 1K, 234M, 2G, etc.).

So, for one example, we can list all files, including hidden ones, in the current directory, sorted by time, in a detailed format by typing

ls -alt shows us

```
drwxr-xr-x  4 root root 4096 Jul 28 02:46  ..
drwx------  3 pi   pi   4096 Jul 10 06:10  .vnc
-rw-------  1 pi   pi    217 Jul 10 06:10  .Xauthority
drwx------ 24 pi   pi   4096 Jul 10 06:09  .config
drwxr-xr-x  2 pi   pi   4096 Jul 10 05:52  Documents
drwxr-xr-x 13 pi   pi   4096 Jul 10 05:46  .cache
drwx------  3 pi   pi   4096 Jul 10 05:07  .pp_backup
drwxr-xr-x  2 pi   pi   4096 Jul  9 08:10  .gstreamer-0.10
drwxr-xr-x  3 pi   pi   4096 Jul  9 08:04  .qmmp
drwxr-xr-x  4 pi   pi   4096 Jul  9 05:25  .audacity-data
```

```
drwxr-xr-x  3 pi    pi    4096 Jul  9 05:21  Dropbox
drwxr-xr-x  2 pi    pi    4096 Jul  9 05:16  Downloads
-rw-r--r--  1 pi    pi    2363 Jul  9 04:10  Main.org
drwx------  2 pi    pi    4096 Jul  6 11:41  .putty
drwxr-xr-x  2 pi    pi    4096 Jul  6 04:28  'Podsafe Music'
-rw-r--r--  1 pi    pi    3795 Jul  6 04:27  .vimrc
-rw-r--r--  1 pi    pi     185 Jul  6 04:27  .tmux.conf
-rw-r--r--  1 pi    pi    1282 Jul  6 04:27  .muttrc
-rw-r--r--  1 pi    pi    8331 Jul  6 04:27  .emacs
drwxr-xr-x  8 pi    pi    4096 Jul  6 04:27  .vim
drwxr-xr-x  4 pi    pi    4096 Jul  6 04:27  .tmux-themepack
drwxr-xr-x  5 pi    pi    4096 Jul  6 04:27  .mutt
drwx------  3 pi    pi    4096 Jul  6 03:54  .gnome
drwx------  3 pi    pi    4096 Jun 20 08:22  .pki
drwxr-xr-x  2 pi    pi    4096 Jun 20 08:20  Music
drwxr-xr-x  2 pi    pi    4096 Jun 20 08:20  Pictures
drwxr-xr-x  2 pi    pi    4096 Jun 20 08:20  Public
drwxr-xr-x  2 pi    pi    4096 Jun 20 08:20  Templates
drwxr-xr-x  2 pi    pi    4096 Jun 20 08:20  Videos
drwxr-xr-x  2 pi    pi    4096 Jun 20 08:20  Desktop
drwx------  3 pi    pi    4096 Jun 20 08:20  .gnupg
drwxr-xr-x  2 pi    pi    4096 Jun 20 07:55  MagPi
drwxr-xr-x  3 pi    pi    4096 Jun 20 07:55  .local
-rw-r--r--  1 pi    pi     220 Jun 20 07:47  .bash_logout
-rw-r--r--  1 pi    pi    3523 Jun 20 07:47  .bashrc
-rw-r--r--  1 pi    pi     807 Jun 20 07:47  .profile
```

You can also include a directory or full path to a directory:

```
ls -al ~
ls -al /home
ls -al /home/brian/Music/Instrumental
```

The Home Directory: ~

The tilde (~) is a special character that represents the current user's "home" folder. This way you can generically reference "home" no matter who you are or where you are in the system.

If you do want to specify a location, you can enter it after the options, like this:

```
ls -al /home/brian/Music
```

This will specifically list the contents of the Music folder for user "brian."

Moving Around in the File System

With the ls command, we learned to see what's in various directories. If you want to move to a directory, you use the cd (*Change Directory*) command.

```
cd /home/brian
```

changes the current directory to the home folder for user brian. Another way to go to the current user's home folder is cd ~. This works even if you don't know the current user's name.

```
cd /
```

takes you to the file system's root, the "root" of the file system "tree." Everything else is a subdirectory branching from /.

```
cd ..
```

Two periods "`..`" represent the directory located just above the current one. For example, if you are in /home/brian/Music right now, and you want to go to /home/brian, you can simply type `cd  ..` and you'll move up one level in the structure. Alternately, you could type `cd /home/brian,` but the two periods are faster to type.

Creating, Deleting, and Listing Directories

Sometimes, you'll need to create a directory/folder, and for that, you use the `mkdir` command. You can create a directory in the current directory by typing

```
mkdir newname
```

or you can make one anywhere in the file system by including a full pathname before the new directory name:

```
mkdir /home/pi/Downloads/newname
```

Note that you have to have access permission in the current directory in order to make a new directory there.

Similarly, to remove a directory, you use the `rmdir` command:

```
rmdir /home/pi/Downloads/newname
```

Removing/deleting a directory requires that the directory be empty. You'll need to delete any files or subdirectories first.

To see a "diagram" of a Linux file system, you can type the command `tree`. It will print a representation of all the subdirectories beneath the path that you indicate. For example, to see the structure of everything in your Downloads directory, you could just type

```
tree ~/Downloads
```

and get the following:

```
/home/pi/Downloads
├── DOS Games Pack.zip
├── kali-linux-2019-2a-rpi3-nexmon-img-xz
│    ├── kali-linux-2019.2a-rpi3-nexmon.img.xz
│    └── kali-linux-2019.2a-rpi3-nexmon.img.xz.txt.sha256sum
└── kali-linux-2019.2a-rpi3-nexmon.img.xz.torrent

1 directory, 4 files
```

Sometimes this can be very useful to see where something is hidden or if there is a directory somewhere you've forgotten about.

In addition to the cd command, you can also use the command pwd to have the system tell you where you are right now. Pwd is short for **Present Working Directory**.

Similarly, if you need to see what the current username is, you can ask whoami, and the system will tell you your current username. If you log in regularly under your own username and additionally use the superuser "pi" account as well, this can sometimes resolve confusion over who the computer thinks you are.

Removing (Deleting) Files

Occasionally, you will want to delete a file. For this, you use the remove command, rm. You always need to follow the rm with some file or directory name:

```
rm /home/brian/junkfile.txt
```

This will delete the file junkfile.txt from my home directory.

```
rm /home/brian/download/*
```

This command uses a "wildcard" character, the asterisk, to denote "everything." This command will delete all the files in the user brian's download directory. This will only delete files, not subdirectories. If you want to delete literally everything in a directory, including everything beneath it, you need the `-r` and `-f` options:

```
rm -rf /home/brian/download/*
```

The `-r` tells `rm` to delete files recursively or, in other words, follow any subdirectories and kill them too. The `-f` option removes confirmation messages. "Are you sure you want to delete this?" kind of messages will no longer appear.

Note that deleting files recursively can be dangerous. The command `rm -rf *` will delete everything on the computer—every system file, every data file, for all users, assuming you have permission to access those files; this is one reason Linux relies on the permissions system. It's much safer than letting every user have complete access to everything.

File Ownership with chown

Speaking of permissions and access, sometimes you may want to change the owner of a file. For example, let's say you created a file, `filename. txt`, as user "pi" and you want to edit it as user "brian." You can load the file into an editor, but when you try to save your changes, you will get a message stating that you don't have permission to do so. Why? Because the operating system thinks it's not your file.

```
sudo chown filename.txt brian
```

This will change the file's ownership to user brian. Note that this requires the "sudo" command to work; this requirement is so not just anyone can change the ownership of files; it has to be someone with responsibility for the system. Remember Linux was created to be a multiple-user operating system with more than one user able to log into the machine, and all this security stuff is designed around that concept.

Copying and Moving Files

It's also very common to copy and move files around from one directory to another. The two commands used here are cp and mv, for copy and move, respectively. The cp command copies a file from one directory to another, and when it's done, there will be a copy of that file in both locations. The mv command does the same thing, but it also deletes the original file, effectively *moving* the file.

```
cp /home/brian/download/game.tar /home/brian
```

will create an exact copy of game.tar in brian's home directory while leaving the original in the download directory.

```
mv /home/brian/download/game.tar /home/brian
```

will create an exact copy of game.tar in brian's home directory and then delete the original in the download directory.

You can also use wildcards to move all files in a folder somewhere.

```
mv ~/download/* ~/backups
```

will move all files in the /home/username/download directory to the /home/username/backups directory.

Man Pages

If in doubt, read the manual! Seriously, one of the things Linux excels at is thorough documentation on command-line apps. If there's a command you don't really understand, you can read a full online manual for it. Let's say Neofetch confuses you; what exactly does it do? What is the purpose?

Assuming you have Neofetch installed, type in

```
man neofetch
```

And you'll get multiple screen pages of documentation, including a synopsis of how to use it, a description explaining the purpose of the app, all the options and parameters that can be used, and anything else that's important. Usually, there's far more information than you may want to know. While reading a manual page, you can use the arrow keys to move up and down, the space bar advances a screen "page," and the Q key on the keyboard quits you back out to the prompt:

```
NEOFETCH(1)                                    User Commands
NAME
       Neofetch - A fast, highly customizable system info script
SYNOPSIS
       neofetch func_name --option "value" --option "value"
DESCRIPTION
       Neofetch  is  a  CLI  system information tool written in
       BASH. Neofetch displays information about
       your system next to an image, your OS logo, or any ASCII
       file of your choice.
       NOTE: Every launch flag has a config option.

OPTIONS
   INFO:
       func_name
                   Specify a function name (second part of info()
                   from config) to quickly  display  only  that
                   function's information.

                   Example: neofetch uptime --uptime_shorthand tiny
                   Example: neofetch uptime disk wm memory
                   This can be used in bars and scripts like so:
                   memory="$(neofetch memory)"; memory="${memory##*:
}"
```

For multiple outputs at once (each line of info
in an array):
IFS=$'\n' read -d "" -ra info < <(neofetch memory
uptime wm)
info=("${info[@]##*: }")
--disable infoname
Allows you to disable an info line from appearing
in the output. 'infoname' is the function
name from the 'print_info()' function inside the
config file. For example: 'info "Memory"
memory' would be '--disable memory'
NOTE: You can supply multiple args. eg. 'neofetch
--disable cpu gpu'

--package_managers on/off
        Hide/Show Package Manager names . (tiny, on, off)

Conclusion

To work on the command line, you're going to need some basic knowledge
of Unix/Linux commands. Still, with the right tools, such as Midnight
Commander or Ranger, you can minimize the need for memorizing and
typing cryptic commands. Another of the terminal's limitations, that it only
shows one app at a time, can be beaten by using Tmux, where you can
literally fill your screen with a dozen simultaneously running apps (not
that getting too many is a good idea, but you **could** do it). Lastly, we looked
at commands used to manipulate files and directories manually from the
command line.

In the next chapter, we'll look at several dozen command-line
programs that will solve many of your work needs. We'll look at email
clients, writing tools, a spreadsheet, and several web browsers, all running
in text mode.

## CHAPTER 6

Using the Command-Line Apps

Now that you can get to a command line and move things around in there, it's time to get some real work done.

In Chapter 4, I showed you the best two or three apps for most tasks. These were all well-known apps that have millions of users, and although some of them have been around a while, they're all still constantly updated and maintained.

In this chapter, I'll show you a few examples of the most common and popular commands to do most tasks, but keep in mind that people have been doing these tasks using similar tools literally for decades (Unix came about in the 1970s, and Linux is directly descended from those tools); there are probably dozens of solutions for each application available, and people are still coming up with new ways of doing the same things. So, after you've looked at my suggestions, do a little Internet research and see if there's some way that fits *your* workflow better.

Writing Tools

Probably the main task for most people (other than maybe browsing the Web and email) is writing. Whether it's simple notes, emails, or full-length books, there are some great text-only tools to do the job.

© Brian Schell 2019
B. Schell, *Computing with the Raspberry Pi*, https://doi.org/10.1007/978-1-4842-5293-2_6

Unlike, say, Microsoft Word or Apple Pages, you can't just highlight a word and make it bold or italic in a text-based terminal window. You usually will need to use some kind of a markup language, such as Markdown or LaTeX (see Chapter 7). Like almost everything else involved with switching to text mode, it's more difficult in the beginning, but far more efficient and speedier once you know how it works.

Nano

Nano Details:

Installation: `sudo apt install nano` (default with Raspian)

Run command: `nano <filename>`

Dotfile: `~/.nanrc`

Help: `man nano`

Web site: `www.nano-editor.org/`

Nano usually comes preinstalled on most Linux systems. It's a really, really basic text editor. In truth, it's almost too basic for most useful tasks—Nano's customization options are very limited. That said, it's almost certainly preinstalled on your system already, and it's fine for quickly reading or making a fast change to a file. Throughout this book, my examples use Nano when we need to edit a text file. It's simple and it's on every system, so that's the "standard" text editor for this book. We've already used Nano a few times in past chapters when adding lines to configuration files. Not only is it fairly simple to learn, but all the functions are easily discoverable via the two-line menu on the bottom of the screen. It's not the "editor of a lifetime," but it may be all you need. There's a markdown version of this chapter visible in Nano in Figure 6-1.

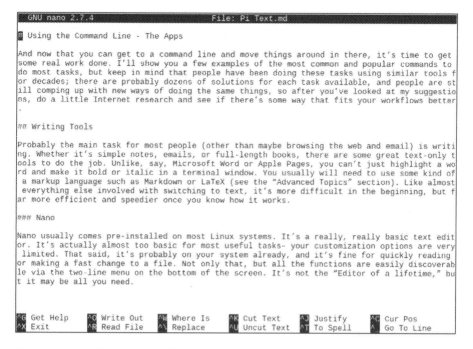

Figure 6-1. *Nano text editor*

Vim

Vim Details:

Installation: `sudo apt install vim`

Run command: `vim <filename>`

Dotfile: `~/.vimrc`

Help: `man vim`

Web site: `www.vim.org/`

Vim and Emacs were designed to be text editors for coders, and if you're a programmer, either of these would be an outstanding choice for you to master. Either one can be adapted for darned near anything, as every single feature you can imagine has myriad customization options and plug-ins.

Vim, at least in my opinion, is a bit harder to learn at first, but well worth it once you get past the learning curve. It's a *modal* editor, meaning that you move around and navigate in one mode, type text in another mode, and visually select things in a third mode. It's an unusual way to work coming from something like Microsoft Word, but there's a lot of power there once you learn how the app works. Vim is shown in Figure 6-2.

```
█ Using the Command Line - The Apps

And now that you can get to a command line and move things around in there, it's time to get some
real work done. I'll show you a few examples of the most common and popular commands to do most
tasks, but keep in mind that people have been doing these tasks using similar tools for decades;
there are probably dozens of solutions for each task available, and people are still comping up with
new ways of doing the same things, so after you've looked at my suggestions, do a little Internet
research and see if there's some way that fits your workflows better.

## Writing Tools

Probably the main task for most people (other than maybe browsing the web and email) is writing.
Whether it's simple notes, emails, or full-length books, there are some great text-only tools to do
the job. Unlike, say, Microsoft Word or Apple Pages, you can't just highlight a word and make it bold
or italic in a terminal window. You usually will need to use some kind of a markup language such as
Markdown or LaTeX (see the "Advanced Topics" section). Like almost everything else involved with
switching to text, it's more difficult in the beginning, but far more efficient and speedier once you
know how it works.

### Nano

Nano usually comes pre-installed on most Linux systems. It's a really, really basic text editor. It's
actually almost too basic for most useful tasks— your customization options are very limited. That
said, it's probably on your system already, and it's fine for quickly reading or making a fast change
to a file. Not only that, but all the functions are easily discoverable via the two-line menu on the
bottom of the screen. It's not the "Editor of a lifetime," but it may be all you need.

 NORMAL  SPELL [EN]    Pi Text.md          markdown   utf-8[unix]   310 words    9%   1/11        1
```

Figure 6-2. *Vim text editor*

Emacs

Emacs Details:

Installation: `sudo apt install emacs25`

Run command: `emacs <filename>`

Dotfile: `~/.emacs`

Help: `man emacs`

Web site: `www.gnu.org/software/emacs/`

Then there's Emacs, as shown in Figure 6-3. There are people who type stuff, check their email, add appointments to their calendars, change their to-do lists, and browse the Web...all without leaving Emacs. It's easier to get started with than Vim, but the more you use it, the deeper the bottomless pit of Emacs becomes. Someone working at the "expert level" of Emacs could probably do everything we talk about in this book...*without leaving Emacs.* There are people who jokingly call Emacs an operating system in itself, but it's so expandable that it's almost not a joke.

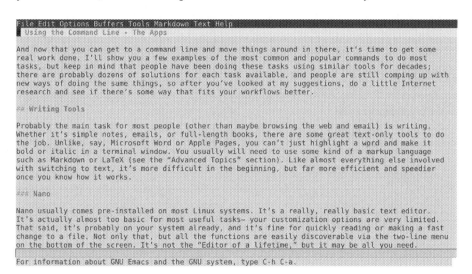

Figure 6-3. *Emacs text editor*

With both Emacs and Vim, nearly any aspect of the editor can be customized and made to work in many different ways. There are also add-ins, themes, and extensions that allow you to do things that even the original developers never imagined that people could in a text editor. For me, it's always been a tough call deciding between these two major writing apps, and I dabble in each, spending far too much time waffling back and forth.

Note that the preceding *apt* command installs *emacs25*, not plain Emacs. You can choose to install the default Emacs, but for some reason, the Raspbian installer will install Emacs version 24 by default, which is a much older, more limited version. Don't use this unless you know some specific reason why you might need it.

WordGrinder

WordGrinder Details:

Installation: `sudo apt install wordgrinder`

Run command: `wordgrinder`

Dotfile: `~/.wordgrinder.lua`

Help: `man wordgrinder`

Web site: `http://cowlark.com/wordgrinder/index.html`

All three of the preceding editors were originally designed with programming/coding in mind. WordGrinder comes at writing from a different perspective. It's a word processor specifically designed for writers. It has easy-to-use menus, the arrow keys work like you'd expect, and there are very few surprises here. You can make words bold or italic easily right in the text, and you don't need to learn Markdown or any special coding.

On the other hand, unlike Emacs or Vim, it's not very customizable; it pretty much works as it comes. There aren't any plug-ins or fancy themes. It's plain, but reliable and simple to use, and it simply works, as you can see in Figure 6-4.

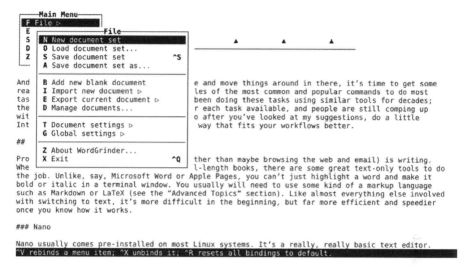

```
  ┌─Main Menu─────────────┐
  │ F File ▷               │
  │ E          ┌─File──────────────────┐
  │ S          │ N New document set     │        ▲        ▲        ▲
  │ D          │ O Load document set... │    ───────────────────────────────
  │ Z          │ S Save document set  ^S│
  │            │ A Save document set as...│
  │ And        │ B Add new blank document │   e and move things around in there, it's time to get some
  │ rea        │ I Import new document ▷  │   les of the most common and popular commands to do most
  │ tas        │ E Export current document ▷│  been doing these tasks using similar tools for decades;
  │ the        │ D Manage documents...    │   r each task available, and people are still comping up
  │ wit        │                          │   o after you've looked at my suggestions, do a little
  │ Int        │ T Document settings ▷    │    way that fits your workflows better.
  │            │ G Global settings ▷      │
  │ ##         │                          │
  │            │ Z About WordGrinder...   │
  │ Pro        │ X Exit              ^Q   │  ther than maybe browsing the web and email) is writing.
  │ Whe        └──────────────────────────┘  l-length books, there are some great text-only tools to do
  the job. Unlike, say, Microsoft Word or Apple Pages, you can't just highlight a word and make it
  bold or italic in a terminal window. You usually will need to use some kind of a markup language
  such as Markdown or LaTeX (see the "Advanced Topics" section). Like almost everything else involved
  with switching to text, it's more difficult in the beginning, but far more efficient and speedier
  once you know how it works.

  ### Nano

  Nano usually comes pre-installed on most Linux systems. It's a really, really basic text editor.
  ^V rebinds a menu item; ^X unbinds it; ^R resets all bindings to default.
```

Figure 6-4. *WordGrinder word processor with easy-to-find menus*

My recommendation is to look at both Nano and WordGrinder first. Nano is great for quick-and-dirty text editing, while WordGrinder can handle most *real* writing tasks. If you decide you really want to become a "text master," then upgrade to the much more powerful and flexible Vim and/or Emacs—they offer far more, but they also require quite a lot of effort to really master.

Email

Probably the primary business use of most computers today, email is a crucial tool. However, due to the prevalence of hackers and spammers, security with email is a major concern. That makes setting up an email client one of the most challenging tasks we're going to run into.

Sendmail

Sendmail Details:

Installation: `sudo apt install sendmail`

Run command: `sendmail`

Dotfile: various files inside /etc/mail

Help: `man sendmail`

Web site: `https://sendmail.org/~ca/email/doc8.12/op.html`

This app is generally a little iffy. Sendmail is a notoriously difficult app to set up, and due to the possibility of being hacked or abused, it's best left to experts. Raspbian's default install does *not* include Sendmail, but other distributions *might* have it already set up and configured, so it's worth giving it a try. Just type a message into a text file, save it, and type something similar to the following:

```
sendmail user@example.com < message.txt
```

Another option would be to try

```
sendmail -t user@example.com
```

and then type your message below that. Hit Ctrl-D to send the message or Ctrl-C to abort. This will either work or it won't depending on the distribution of Linux you are running. Again, I recommend that if this doesn't "just work" out of the box for you, you move on to other options, as it's a powerful but dangerously complex app to configure.

Mutt

Mutt Details:

Installation: `sudo apt install mutt`

Run command: `mutt`

Dotfile: `~/.muttrc`

Help: `man mutt`

Web site: `www.mutt.org/`

Mutt (and Alpine, in the following) is a much more complete email client than Sendmail. You get a full interface to search, sort, read, and reply to your emails; and it's easy to deal with multiple folders and message attachments. Which you choose depends on what you need and which one you find more attractive and usable. They both do pretty much the same things.

One major disadvantage that I have found with Mutt is that it stores your passwords in the configuration files in plain text. If anyone got into your system, they could easily look at your email passwords and cause you a world of trouble. You *can* use Mutt and have it not store the passwords, but then you would need to reenter your email password every time you load Mutt, which is inconvenient, to say the least.

Still, for a text-based app, it's attractive, includes some menuing options onscreen, and isn't too hard to set up. Figure 6-5 shows an email from a blog I write for.

Figure 6-5. *Mutt email client*

Alpine

Alpine Details:

Installation: `sudo apt install alpine`

Run command: `alpine`

Dotfile: `~/.pinerc`

Help: `man alpine`

Web site: `http://alpine.x10host.com/alpine/`

Alpine doesn't have the same ease of customization that Mutt has, but it does have the ability to store encrypted passwords on the server. If you have a remote system (i.e., you SSH into it) and you don't want to be bothered typing your email password every time, this is the better option. It also can be configured from within the app via menus, while Mutt relies on figuring out how to modify a "dotfile," which we'll talk about later. Figure 6-6 will give you a hint of the menuing aspect of Alpine.

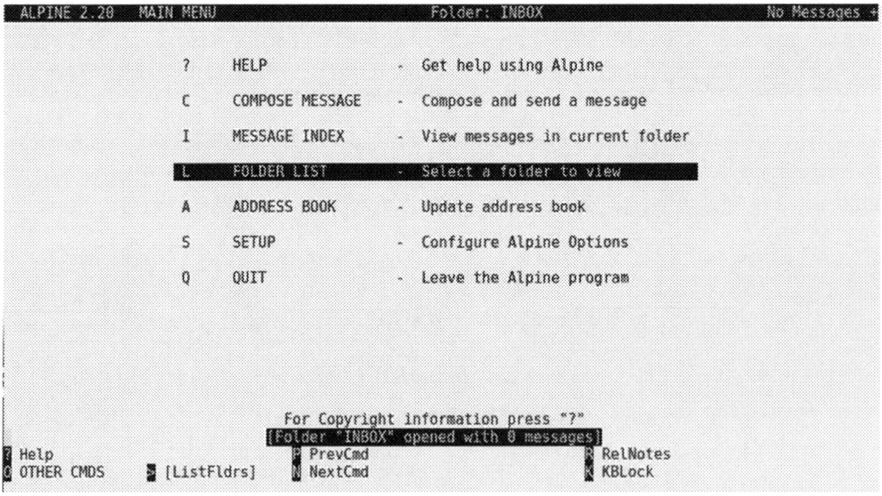

Figure 6-6. *Alpine email client*

Other "Office" Apps

Writing and email are a big deal for most of us, but a great deal of useful work also involves numbers and presentations. In the GUI world, there is Microsoft Excel and PowerPoint, or even LibreOffice. Those don't work on the command line, so we need to find something similar.

SC and SC-IM

SC Details:

Installation: `sudo apt install sc`

Run command: `sc`

Dotfile: `~/.scrc`

Help: `man sc`

Web site: `https://github.com/n-t-roff/sc`

SC is short for Screen Calculator, otherwise known as the spreadsheet for text mode. It does all the basic stuff that spreadsheets like Excel do, but does it all through the keyboard and text screen. It wants to save all its files in CSV (comma-separated values), but it can read in Excel files. It allows right and left text alignment, cut and paste, and various decimal formatting options as well as a huge number of calculation and math functions. It's not as pretty as a GUI spreadsheet, but the power is all there. If you remember back to the days of VisiCalc or Lotus 1-2-3, this will bring back either fond memories or nightmares.

The original SC program was created around 13 years ago; the SC-IM fork is still being developed and maintained, so even though it looks like it's straight from the 1980s, it's safe and well maintained. Figure 6-7 shows a simple calculation of totaling and averaging a column of numbers.

```
sudo apt install sc
```

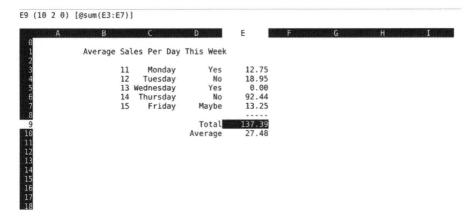

Figure 6-7. *SC spreadsheet calculator*

You can find out more at these links:

- SC spreadsheet calculator article: `www.linuxjournal.com/article/10699`

- SC mini manual: `www.adrianjwells.freeuk.com/minmansc.pdf`

Presentations

Out in the world of Windows and Mac, PowerPoint, Keynote, Impress, or even Google Slides are available for presentations. Slideshow presentations *scream* for graphics, so a text-based presentation may not be the best way to go most of the time. Still, sometimes you want to do something just to show that you *can* do a thing, so here are your presentation options: Beamer, Vimdeck, and MDP.

Beamer isn't an *app* per se; it's an extension of LaTeX (see Chapter 7) that allows you to create a file using a text editor and then output it as a PDF that can be shown on a projector, printed out, or emailed to recipients. It allows colored text, graphics, diagrams, and basically any kind of media

138

that is supported by LaTeX. It doesn't do any kind of animation, as it outputs in PDF, but any static imagery can be used.

Beamer Details:

Installation: `sudo apt install latex-beamer` (note: requires texlive-full and texmaker to be already installed)

Run command: `load the output into your PDF viewer`

Dotfile: `none`

Help: `www.overleaf.com/learn/latex/Beamer_Presentations:_A_Tutorial_for_Beginners_(Part_1)%E2%80%94Getting_Started`

Web site: `https://github.com/josephwright/beamer`

Vimdeck is a tool that allows you to write a file using Markdown (see Chapter 7) and compile it into a presentation that can be viewed using Vim. You don't have to use Vim to create the file, but the final presentation is optimized for use within Vim. The "slide" in Figure 6-8 is actually just a page within a big text file displayed in Vim.

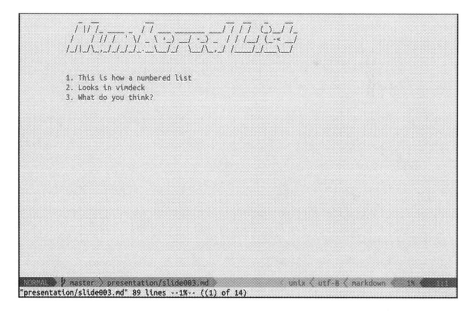

Figure 6-8. *Vimdeck presentation*

Vimdeck Details:

Installation: `sudo gem install vimdeck`

Run command: `vimdeck`

Dotfile: none

Help: `vimdeck`

Web site: `https://github.com/tybenz/vimdeck`

MDP is an app that runs a presentation in text. Beamer and Vimdeck were tools to create presentation files, while MDP takes markdown text and does the actual presentation (see Figure 6-9), with lots of nice options including color, citations, headers, nested lists, and lots of other text-based (still no graphics) elements.

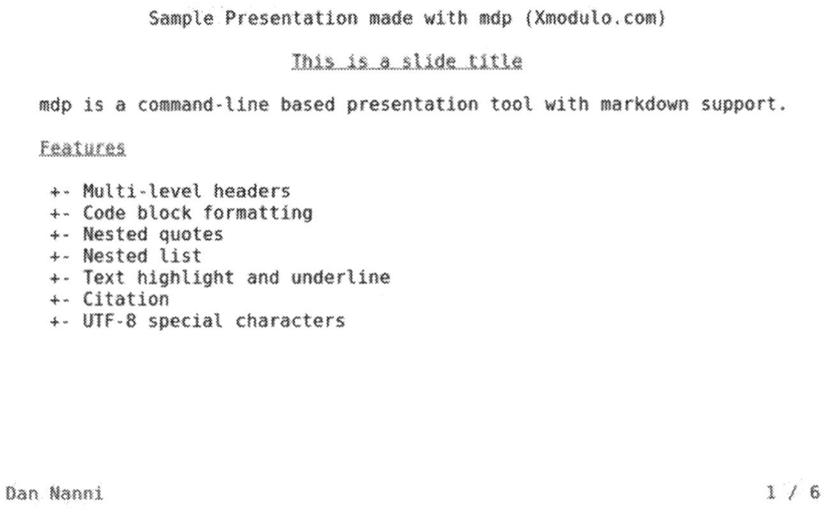

```
            Sample Presentation made with mdp (Xmodulo.com)

                       This is a slide title

    mdp is a command-line based presentation tool with markdown support.

    Features

        +- Multi-level headers
        +- Code block formatting
        +- Nested quotes
        +- Nested list
        +- Text highlight and underline
        +- Citation
        +- UTF-8 special characters




    Dan Nanni                                                    1 / 6
```

Figure 6-9. *MDP presentation*

MDP Details:

Installation: `sudo apt install mdp`

Run command: `mdp`

Dotfile: none

Help: `man mdp`

Web site: `https://github.com/visit1985/mdp`

Notes Apps

Making quick notes is one of the things GUI operating systems excel at, but sometimes you need to copy some text for later or make a detailed note for another time and you don't want to leave the command line. We'll look at two major players here: Terminal Velocity is an app that makes it super quick to jot down and find text-based notes, while Emacs Org-mode is an outliner, scheduler, to-do manager, and complete organizing system built into the word processor Emacs.

Terminal Velocity

Terminal Velocity is a fairly recent app inspired by the Mac OSX app called Notational Velocity. To create a new note, type a title for the note and hit Enter. The note will be opened in your text editor. As you type the title, the list of notes filters to show notes that match what you've typed, giving you a chance to open a related note instead of making a new one. This means that you use the same line to type a new note as you do to search for an existing one, which makes the whole process of searching and creating very fast. I use this one in conjunction with Dropbox to keep my notes with me on all my devices.

Terminal Velocity is installed differently from other apps we've looked at, as it's not in the Raspbian repositories. We'll use an app called *Pip* to install it.

Terminal Velocity Details:
Installation: `sudo pip install terminal-velocity`
Run command: `terminal_velocity`
Dotfile: `~/.tvrc`
Help: `see web site`
Web site: `https://vhp.github.io/terminal_velocity/`

Emacs Org-mode

We've already discussed Emacs in the "Writing Tools" section, but it deserves another mention here. "Org-mode" is a special mode that Emacs offers that allows you to type in text that is viewed as a sort of outline. You write files in a format similar to Markdown; but you can also use the Tab key to quickly collapse or expand outline trees, move whole sections up and down, and quickly create things like to-do lists, outlines, and notes of all kinds. If you already have some familiarity with Emacs, it's easy to get started using Org-mode, but there is so much you can do with it that the options can get extensive.

Figure 6-10 shows my to-do list for June 13. Even without explaining how the to-do format works in Org-mode, you can understand exactly what's going on in the file.

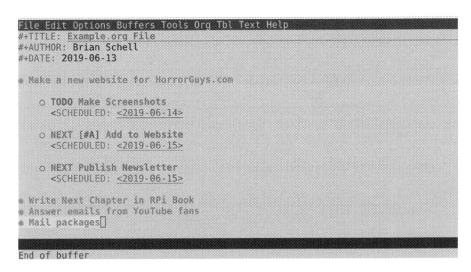

Figure 6-10. *Emacs Org-mode file*

Security

One thing you don't generally have to worry about when using Linux is viruses. Due to the way everything is split up and restricted by usernames and permissions, it's much harder to catch a virus than on, say, a Windows machine. That does not, however, mean you don't still have to be concerned about security. One major area of concern worth looking at is password security.

Pass

Pass is a password management system. It can keep track of a database of thousands of web sites and passwords and is especially useful in creating secure passwords. You can request a new password, specifying the number of symbols, and it generates what you need completely randomly and copies it to the clipboard.

This kind of app is tremendously helpful. I've gone from weak passwords such as

```
USER: brianschell
PASSWORD: PENCIL (or the cat's name or something)
```

to

```
USER: brianschell
PASSWORD: zagw@JPTfVquVkQjvAetx2ZiA
```

Obviously, a password like that is hard, if not impossible, to remember—or type for that matter; fortunately, Pass will copy the password into the clipboard for you.

Pass Details:

Installation: `sudo apt install pass`

Run command: `pass`

Dotfile: none

Help: `man pass`

Web site: `www.passwordstore.org`

Also, a *Pass* installation and tutorial can be found at `www.2daygeek.com/pass-command-line-password-manager-linux/`.

rTorrent

rTorrent Details:

Installation: `sudo apt install rtorrent`

Run command: `rtorrent`

Dotfile: `~/.rtorrent.rc`

Help: `man rtorrent`

Web site: `http://rakshasa.github.io/rtorrent/`

As I mentioned back in Chapters 3 and 4, when we talked about the Deluge app, BitTorrent gets a lot of bad press for being one method people use to share "pirated" files, but it has many legitimate uses as well. Many alternative Linux distributions are available via torrent, and it's actually a very efficient means of transferring large files.

In order to download files distributed through torrents, you need a torrent client. There are many good ones available for the GUI (we already talked about Deluge), but sometimes it's nice to be able to do it from the command line. We'll look at one app called rTorrent here.

You will also need at least one `.torrent` file to download. One good place to find legal torrents is at `www.offensive-security.com/kali-linux-arm-images/`, and if you go there, you can find something to download, even if it's only to test the system. The file I downloaded was `kali-linux-2019.2a-rpi3-nexmon.img.xz.torrent`, a Linux distribution for the Raspberry Pi that I've never tried before.

Start the rTorrent app by typing `rtorrent` at the command line. It will then run in full-screen mode, as in Figure 6-11.

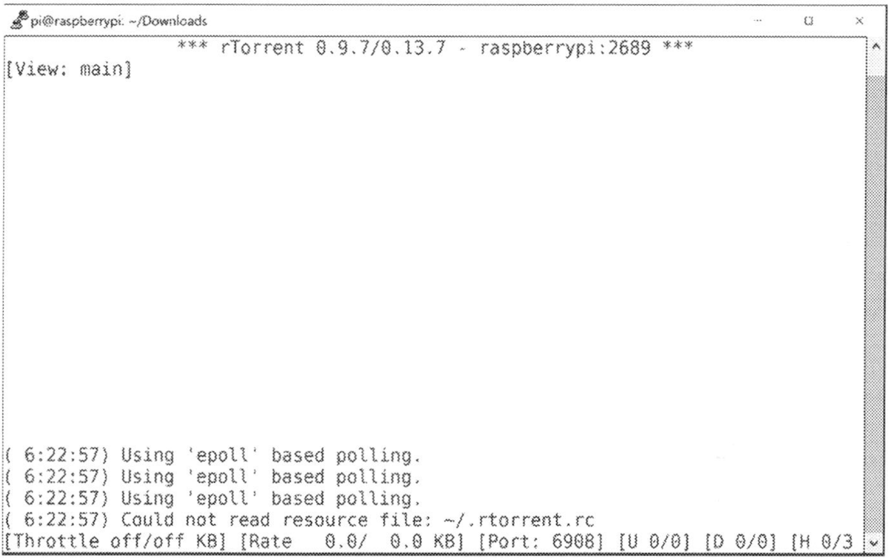

```
pi@raspberrypi: ~/Downloads                                              ...    □    ×
                    *** rTorrent 0.9.7/0.13.7 - raspberrypi:2689 ***
[View: main]




















( 6:22:57) Using 'epoll' based polling.
( 6:22:57) Using 'epoll' based polling.
( 6:22:57) Using 'epoll' based polling.
( 6:22:57) Could not read resource file: ~/.rtorrent.rc
[Throttle off/off KB] [Rate    0.0/   0.0 KB] [Port: 6908] [U 0/0] [D 0/0] [H 0/3
```

Figure 6-11. *rTorrent running in full-screen mode*

Next, hit the Enter key, and it will give you a prompt, load.normal>, at
the bottom of the screen, just like in Figure 6-12.

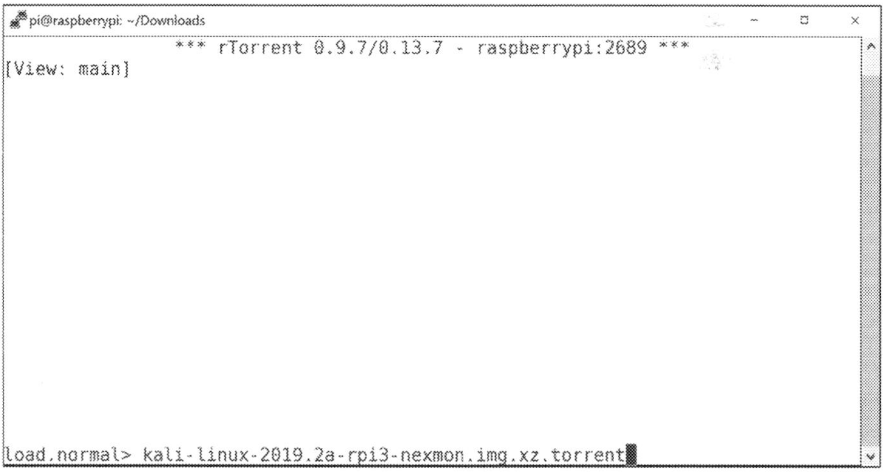

```
pi@raspberrypi: ~/Downloads                                              –    □    ×
                    *** rTorrent 0.9.7/0.13.7 - raspberrypi:2689 ***
[View: main]

















load.normal> kali-linux-2019.2a-rpi3-nexmon.img.xz.torrent█
```

Figure 6-12. *Adding the .torrent file*

You will need to be sure to type (or cut and paste) the entire filename exactly correctly. Hit Enter, and the file will appear in the main section of the screen, the active torrent list, as shown near the top of Figure 6-13.

```
pi@raspberrypi: ~/Downloads                                    ...    ▭    ×
                *** rTorrent 0.9.7/0.13.7 - raspberrypi:2689 ***
[View: main]
   kali-linux-2019-2a-rpi3-nexmon-img-xz
   [CLOSED]     0.0 / 892.6 MB Rate:   0.0 /   0.0 KB Uploaded:     0.0 MB
   Inactive:




[Throttle off/off KB] [Rate   0.0/  0.0 KB] [Port: 6908] [U 0/0] [D 0/0] [H 0/3
```

Figure 6-13. *rTorrent with one torrent added*

You can add as many .torrent files as you wish this way. rTorrent can easily support hundreds of torrents if that's something you want to deal with. You can move through the list of torrents with the up and down arrow keys to select individual torrents.

Ctrl-O changes the destination directory. I prefer ~/Downloads, but you can put your files wherever you like. The default is the user's root directory.

Ctrl-S starts the download. You can watch the numbers and statistics at the bottom of the screen to see how things are progressing.

Ctrl-D pauses the download. If you hit Ctrl-D a second time, the download will be deleted.

The `right arrow` allows you get information about the files being downloaded.

`Ctrl-K` allows you to close a torrent.

For more information and documentation on all the features of rTorrent, their web site is at `https://rakshasa.github.io/rtorrent/`.

Web Browsers

Wait—browsing the Web in text mode? Yes, you can!

The following three browsers have all been around for decades, and all three have the ability to deal with mostly-text web sites. Some allow for image viewing through external viewers, while some allow in-line image viewing with plug-ins. None are as robust or pretty as modern GUI browsers, but they often can get the job done.

There *are* benefits to using text-mode browsers. First, they are blazing fast compared to graphical browsers—they don't run the embedded JavaScript codes, and they don't download all those images (including the invisible tracking images). Since all they do is download the text, they're fast even on a slow system. Also, because they're text-only, they allow easy integration with text-to-speech software and work very well for the visually impaired.

Googler

Googler Details:

Installation: `sudo apt install googler`

Run command: `googler <keywords>`

Dotfile: (none)

Help: `man googler`

Web site: `https://github.com/jarun/googler`

Sometimes you don't want to open a full web browser to check something on Google, but in the GUI world, that's the only way to do it. Not so with the command line! The little app "Googler" will let you type in your search phrase right on the command line, and it'll show you multiple results with short little abstracts about what Google has found. If you see something you want, then you have the option of loading it in a browser.

Lynx

Lynx Details:

Installation: `sudo apt install lynx`

Run command: `lynx <URL>`

Dotfile: `~/.lynxrc`

Help: `man lynx`

Web site: `https://lynx.browser.org/`

This is the oldest of the browsers, as it was first begun as a project in 1992. Due to this longevity, it's quite stable and safe. It doesn't work with sites requiring JavaScript but does handle sites with cookies.

As shown in Figure 6-14, it can take a regular web site, strip out the graphical elements, and reformat everything so it shows up entirely on a text-based screen. This is very similar to how certain assistive technologies allow blind people to use the Web, as the resulting text can easily be channeled into a screen reader.

```
}
   ▓Brian Schell's Home » Feed Brian Schell's Home » Comments Feed Brian Schell's Home » About Brian Sc
hell Comments Feed alternate
      alternate

Brian Schell's Home

   Your Favorite Author, Editor, and Narrator

      * Home
      * Brian's Blog
      * Amateur Radio
          + DMR For Beginners: Using the Tytera MD-380
          + FM Satellite Communications for Beginners
          + D-Star for Beginners Second Edition
          + OpenSpot for Beginners: D-Star, Fusion, and DMR Accessed Easily
          + SDR for Beginners Using the SDRplay and SDRuno
          + Echolink for Beginners Second Edition
          + Programming Amateur Radios with CHIRP Ham Radio Setups Made Easy
      * Technology
          + Going Chromebook: Living in the Cloud
          + Going Chromebook: Learn to Master Google Docs
          + DOS Today: Running Vintage MS-DOS Games and Apps on a Modern Computer
          + Going Text: Mastering the Power of the Command Line
          + Going iPad: Making the iPad Your Only Computer
-- press space for next page --
   Arrow keys: Up and Down to move.  Right to follow a link; Left to go back.
H)elp O)ptions P)rint G)o M)ain screen Q)uit /=search [delete]=history list
```

Figure 6-14. *Lynx browser*

W3M

W3M Details:

Installation: sudo apt install w3m (Raspian preinstalled)

Run command: w3m <URL>

Dotfile: ~/.w3m/config

Help: man w3m

Web site: http://w3m.sourceforge.net/

W3M is also quite old, begun in 1995. It has support for tables, frames, SSL connections, color, and inline images on suitable terminals. Generally, it renders pages in a form as true to their original layout as possible. W3M is one of the more actively maintained browsers and has many extensions and plug-ins, so this may be the best choice if you need to do a lot of text-based web use.

Figure 6-15 shows the W3M rendering of the same web site as in Figure 6-14's Lynx browser. Compare the differences.

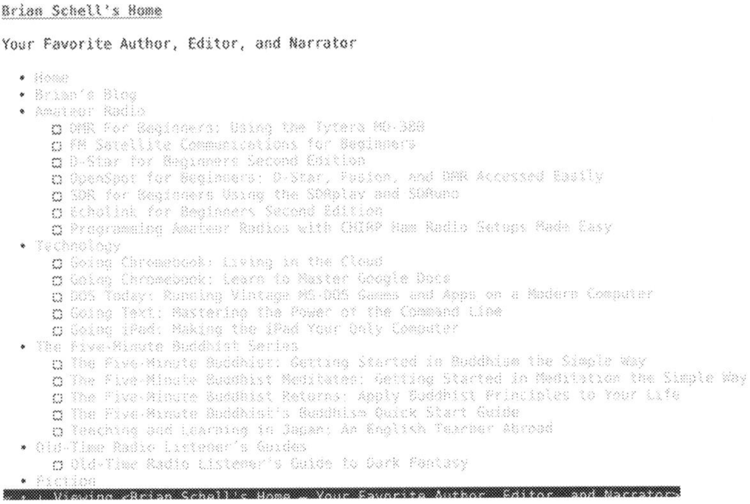

Brian Schell's Home

Your Favorite Author, Editor, and Narrator

- Home
- Brian's Blog
- Amateur Radio
  - DMR for Beginners: Using the Tytera MD-380
  - FM Satellite Communications for Beginners
  - D-Star for Beginners Second Edition
  - OpenSpot for Beginners: D-Star, Fusion, and DMR Accessed Easily
  - SDR for Beginners Using the SDRplay and SDRuno
  - Echolink for Beginners Second Edition
  - Programming Amateur Radios with CHIRP Ham Radio Setups Made Easy
- Technology
  - Going Chromebook: Living in the Cloud
  - Going Chromebook: Learn to Master Google Docs
  - DOS Today: Running Vintage MS-DOS Games and Apps on a Modern Computer
  - Going Text: Mastering the Power of the Command Line
  - Going iPad: Making the iPad Your Only Computer
- The Five-Minute Buddhist Series
  - The Five-Minute Buddhist: Getting Started in Buddhism the Simple Way
  - The Five-Minute Buddhist Meditates: Getting Started in Meditation the Simple Way
  - The Five-Minute Buddhist Returns: Apply Buddhist Principles to Your Life
  - The Five-Minute Buddhist's Buddhism Quick Start Guide
  - Teaching and Learning in Japan: An English Teacher Abroad
- Old-Time Radio Listener's Guides
  - Old-Time Radio Listener's Guide to Dark Fantasy
- Fiction

Viewing «Brian Schell's Home — Your Favorite Author, Editor, and Narrator»

Figure 6-15. *W3M browser*

ELinks

ELinks Details:

Installation: sudo apt install elinks

Run command: elinks <URL>

Dotfile: ~/.elinks

Help: man elinks

Web site: http://elinks.or.cz/

This is the most "modern-looking" of the three browsers, as you can see in Figure 6-16. It has a color display, and when you press the Esc key, navigation menus appear that make the whole thing easier to figure out. It supports the mouse, tabs, cookies, and more.

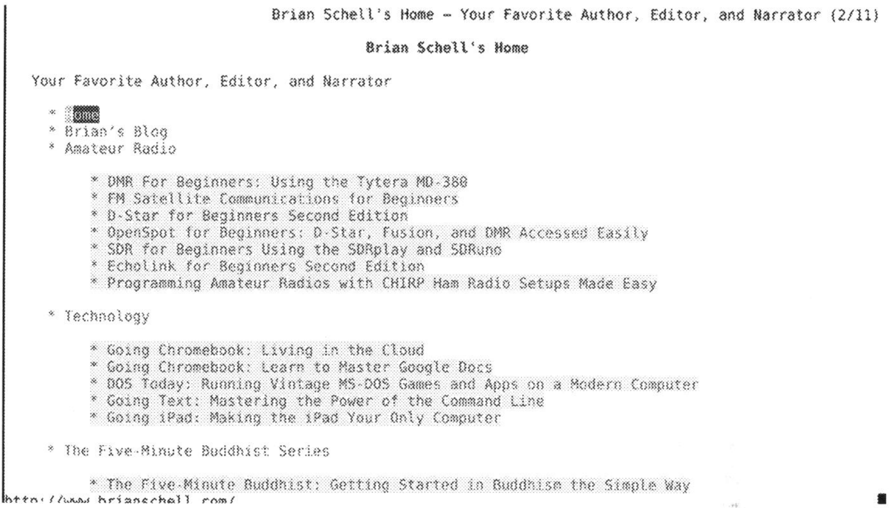

Figure 6-16. ELinks browser

Communications

One of the most popular things to do back when the Internet started becoming available to everyone was to hang out in IRC chat rooms. Before Facebook, before Twitter, even back before MySpace, there was IRC (Internet Relay Chat).

IRC: WeeChat and IRSSI

WeeChat Details:

Installation: `sudo apt install weechat`

Run command: `weechat`

Dotfile: `~/.weechat`

Help: `man weechat`

Web site: `https://weechat.org/`

IRSSI Details:

Installation: `sudo apt install irssi`

151

Run command: `irssi`

Dotfile: `~/.irssi/config`

Help: `man irssi`

Web site: `https://irssi.org/`

Believe it or not, IRC is still very popular and still going strong, especially among the tech community. There are numerous ways to get on IRC, even through the command line. Both of the apps presented here, WeeChat and IRSSI, are actively developed and going strong. Figure 6-17 shows WeeChat, but both apps are similar to the picture.

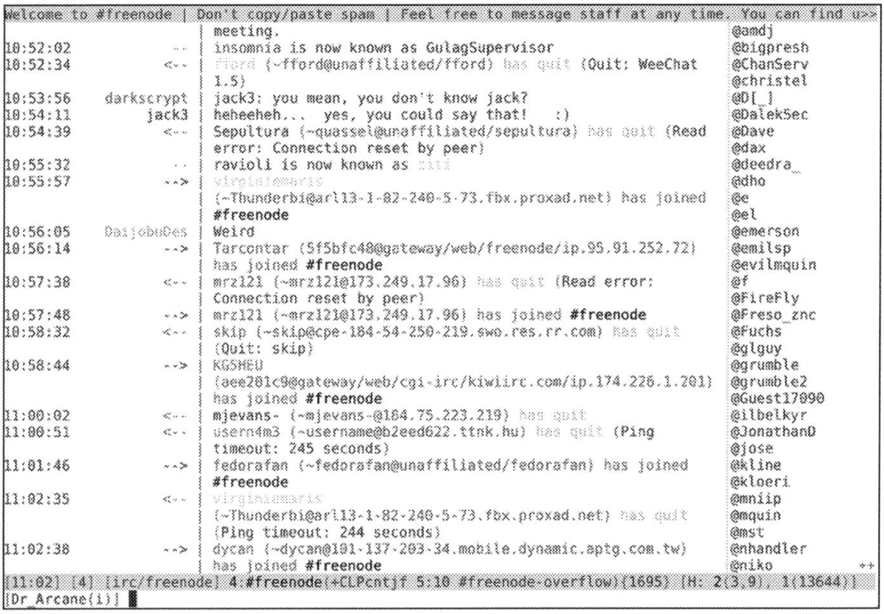

Figure 6-17. *WeeChat IRC client*

Both offer scripting, plug-ins, themes, filters, help screens, and everything else you need to get started.

VOIP

As far as I know, there is no command-line replacement for Skype, FaceTime, or other VOIP software. There is an "experimental" project called Twinkle that exists but is reported to be crash-prone and unreliable.

If this is something you badly need, you might want to take a look. The app comes from `https://github.com/LubosD/twinkle`.

Social Media

Most command-line apps are actively developed versions of apps that were originally created decades ago. Social media is a relatively new area of computing, and the command line has a ways to go to catch up here. Also, most social media sites rely heavily on graphics, and obviously, that's not a great match for text mode. Still, there are a few good apps out there, and remember you can easily access most social media sites through one of the text-based web browsers if necessary.

Twitter

Rainbow Stream Details:

Installation: `sudo pip install rainbowstream`

Run command: `rainbowstream`

Dotfile: `~/.rainbow_config.json`

Help: `Hit "h" in the app`

Web site: `https://github.com/orakaro/rainbowstream`

You wouldn't think Twitter clients would be all that hard to come by, but there's only one that I could really recommend: **Rainbow Stream**. It's easy to install and configure, and it allows you to post and narrow the stream into list view and does almost anything else you would want to do with Twitter.

Of course, you can use Twitter through any of the text-based web browsers by going to `http://twitter.com` instead of using a specialized client app.

Facebook

There's not a "regular" Facebook client for the command line, but you can use their site through any of the text-based web browsers. There is, however, a command-line client for Facebook *Messenger*.

```
sudo apt install npm
sudo npm install -g fb-messenger-cli
```

Graphics, Art, and Photos

You wouldn't think graphics and art would even be a category in the world of text, but there are some excellent tools to work on images, even from text mode. Asciiview is just a fun app to create "pictures" using only text characters. FIGlet is a fun little thing that lets you create text banners, and ImageMagick is a monstrous tool that can do nearly anything involving changing graphic formats and editing pictures—without even seeing them.

Asciiview

Asciiview Details:

Installation: `sudo apt install aview`

Run command: `aview <filename.bpm>`

Dotfile: `none`

Help: `man aview`

Web site: `http://aa-project.sourceforge.net/tune/`

For years, our cameras have been advertising more and more megapixels. Sometimes, once in a while, it's more fun to go the other way around and look for the *lowest* resolutions possible. One of those cases would be when you need to display a photograph or graphic image on a text-only terminal.

One way to get this done is to use Asciiview. Figure 6-18 is a photo of me run through Asciiview, which was then converted into textual symbols. If you look closely, you will see that there are no graphic characters at all; it's just letters, numbers, and symbols.

Figure 6-18. *The author's photo in Asciiview*

To convert an image, type

```
aview myphoto.bpm
```

FIGlet

FIGlet Details:

Installation: `sudo apt install figlet`

Run command: `figlet <text string>`

Dotfile: none

Help: `man figlet`

Web site: `www.figlet.org/`

FIGlet is just a little command-line tool to take a line of text and make a sort of textual "banner" from it. You can enter a single word or a whole sentence, depending on your needs. For example,

```
figlet Brian
```

will then return

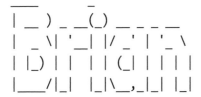

ImageMagick

ImageMagick Details:

Installation: `sudo apt install imagemagick`

Run command(s): `convert, identify, mogrify, compare, montage, composite, display,` and so on. **It's a suite of commands.**

Dotfile: none

Help: `man imagemagick`

Web site: www.imagemagick.org/

Both the preceding Ascii apps are little more than toys. Sometimes you need to actually do some graphical work, and for that, there's ImageMagick.

The full documentation for ImageMagick is at

www.imagemagick.org/script/command-line-processing.php.

It includes tools to create, edit, compose, or convert bitmap images. It can read and write images in over 200 formats, including PNG, JPEG, GIF, HEIC, TIFF, DPX, EXR, WebP, Postscript, PDF, and SVG.

You can use ImageMagick to resize, flip, mirror, rotate, distort, shear, and transform images, adjust image colors, apply various special effects, or draw text, lines, polygons, ellipses, and Bézier curves.

The ImageMagick command-line tools can be as simple as this, which converts and image in jpg format to the same image in png format:

```
convert image.jpg image.png
```

Or it can be outrageously complex with a plethora of options, as in the following:

```
convert -delay 100 -size 100x100 xc:SkyBlue -page
+5+10  balloon.gif -page +35+30 medical.gif -page +62+50
present.gif -page +10+55 shading.gif -loop 0  animation.gif
```

Audio and Video

The computer can get boring at times with just text on the screen. Fortunately, you don't have to sit there and work in silence. Computers were playing music long before GUI interfaces, and you can play all your music with command-line tools. It's actually even easier to create playlists and automate your music using these tools. If you want to watch a movie while you work, that's completely possible too.

Music Players

The Raspberry Pi has excellent hardware for playing music, either through the audio jack or through HDMI. The command line has numerous excellent (and very customizable) music players. My two favorites are MOC and CMUS.

Both work better if you have your music library organized in individual artist directories. At one point, I had all my music in Apple iTunes; so I just downloaded all the songs from there, copied the giant "Music" folder to its own directory, and pointed the music players at them—the default organization leftover from iTunes works without any modification. I'm not saying you **need** iTunes to organize your music, but a lot of people already have that somewhere, and if you do, it's one easy way to go.

MOC (Music on Console)

MOC Details:

Installation: `sudo apt install moc`

Run command: `mocp`

Dotfile: `~/.moc/config`

Help: `man moc`

Web site: `http://moc.daper.net/`

I like this one, especially when I am working with a playlist. It has two columns, and the default layout looks a lot like the Midnight Commander app. As Figure 6-19 shows, you can see your music files on the left pane, and the playlist you are working with lives in the right pane. Select a file and "add" it to the list, and you can visually see what you're doing. It's theme-able and has an equalizer built in, the keys can be remapped to your preferences, and it even has support for Internet streams. It's got a convenient help screen; just hit "H," and all the commands will pop up for you.

Figure 6-19. *MOC (Music on Console)*

Run the MOC player with `mocp` (note the p at the end).

CMUS (C Music Player)

CMUS Details:

Installation: `sudo apt install cmus`

Run command: `cmus`

Dotfile: `/usr/share/cmus/rc`

Help: `man cmus`

Web site: `https://cmus.github.io/`

While MOC is great for working with playlists, I like CMUS better
for just browsing and playing songs on a whim (see Figure 6-20); the
navigation feels nicer to me. While MOC has a navigation system
reminiscent of **Midnight Commander**, CMUS looks and feels more like
Ranger. Your choice of music player may be closely related to which file
browsing system you prefer.

```
Library ~/.config/cmus/lib.pl - 39 tracks sorted by albumartist date album discnumber tracknumber tit
/home/brian/Music/Apocalyptica/Apocalyptica/09 Betrayal   Forgiveness.m4a                      05:13
Apocalyptica          1. Enter Sandman (edit)                                                   03:32
Apocalyptica          2. Enter Sandman (album version)                                          03:41
Apocalyptica          1. Path                                                          2001 03:06
Apocalyptica          2. Struggle                                                      2001 03:27
Apocalyptica          3. Romance                                                       2001 03:27
Apocalyptica          4. Pray!                                                         2001 04:24
Apocalyptica          5. In Memoriam                                                   2001 04:42
Apocalyptica          6. Hyperventilation                                              2001 04:29
Apocalyptica          7. Beyond Time                                                   2001 03:57
Apocalyptica          8. Hope                                                          2001 03:25
Apocalyptica          9. Kaamos                                                        2001 04:41
Apocalyptica         10. Coma                                                          2001 06:45
Apocalyptica         11. Hall of the Mountain King                                     2001 03:29
Apocalyptica         12. Until It Sleeps                                               2001 03:14
Apocalyptica         13. Fight Fire With Fire                                          2001 03:27
Apocalyptica         14. Path, Volume 2 (feat. Sandra Nasic)                           2001 03:23
Apocalyptica         15. Hope, Volume 2 (feat. Matthias Sayer)                         2001 04:01
Apocalyptica         16. Harmageddon (live in Munich)                                  2001 05:06
Apocalyptica         17. Nothing Else Matters (live in Munich)                         2001 05:23
Apocalyptica         18. Inquisition Symphony (live in Munich)                         2001 05:15
Apocalyptica          1. Life Burns!                                                   2005 03:06
Apocalyptica          2. Quutamo                                                       2005 03:26
Apocalyptica          3. Distraction                                                   2005 03:53
Apocalyptica          4. Bittersweet                                                   2005 04:26
Apocalyptica          5. Misconstruction                                              2005 03:56
Apocalyptica - Enter Sandman - 1. Enter Sandman (edit)
> 00:09 / 03:32 - 2:39:18 vol: 100                                       all from library | C
```

Figure 6-20. *CMUS (C Music Player)*

CMUS supports most music formats from the default install: Ogg
Vorbis, MP3, FLAC, Opus, Musepack, WavPack, WAV, AAC, MP4, audio CD,
and everything supported by ffmpeg (WMA, APE, MKA, TTA, SHN, etc.)
and libmodplug. If you get your music from various sources, then being
able to not worry about your format being understood is a nice plus.

Like MOC, CMUS has remappable keys, theming, and color
customizing. This one, however, also allows for music streaming
from online radio stations if you can find the url for the stream, that is,
http://beirutnights.com/live.m3u.

Install with sudo apt install cmus.

MPC/MPD (Music Player Daemon/Controller)

MPD Details:

Installation: sudo apt install mpd

Run command: mpd

Dotfile: /etc/mpd.conf

Help: `man mpd`

Web site: `www.musicpd.org`

Both of the previous entries, MOC and CMUS, were full-screen apps that relied heavily on visually navigating files and directories. Both interfaces were inspired by file management systems, and both are at least somewhat interactive with their controls.

An alternative is the Music Player Daemon, or MPD. It is a flexible, powerful, server-side application for playing music. Through plug-ins and libraries, it can play a variety of sound files while being controlled by its network protocol. Since it's a *daemon*, it just runs **silently** in the background and waits for commands from an external client program.

MPC is the parallel client app. It connects to MPD and controls it according to commands and arguments passed to it. If no arguments are passed, current status is given. It's strictly a command-line tool, with no visuals whatsoever.

There are, however, a number of *other* clients that work with the MPD server. Some are graphical, some are for the Web, while others are for use on the console. It's a bit harder to set up, but it's *very* flexible and powerful.

MPD Daemon home page: `www.musicpd.org/`

MPD clients: `www.musicpd.org/clients/`

Essentially the point of MPD is that with the client/server architecture, you can set up one machine in your house with all the music files stored on it and then access and play that music from other computers located on the network without storing your music files in multiple places.

Movie Viewers

Movies are obviously visual. The old-style terminals and computers back in the early days of Unix couldn't play video files because the monitors just couldn't handle it. Your Raspberry Pi, on the other hand, can play movies easily. The model 4 Pi can even handle *dual* 4K outputs. These systems can play videos, and there's no real reason why you cannot play your movies from the command line.

MPlayer

MPlayer Details:

Installation: `sudo apt install mplayer`

Run command: `mplayer <filename>`

Dotfile: various files inside `/etc/mplayer/`

Help: `man mplayer`

Web site: `www.mplayerhq.hu/`

MPlayer is a movie player which runs on many systems. It plays most MPEG/VOB, AVI, Ogg/OGM, VIVO, ASF, WMA, WMV, QT, MOV, MP4, RealMedia, Matroska, NUT, NuppelVideo, FLI, YUV4MPEG, FILM, RoQ, and PVA files, supported by many native, XAnim, and Win32 DLL codecs. You can watch VideoCD, SVCD, DVD, 3ivx, DivX 3/4/5, WMV, and even H.264 movies.

In most cases, you can enjoy movies either in full-screen mode or in a window. There's a screenshot of the title of a movie beginning in Figure 6-21.

Figure 6-21. *MPlayer status on the left, MPlayer movie on the right*

Even with all this, you still may prefer to watch your videos in the GUI with an app like VLC (discussed elsewhere), but it's good to know you have the ability to watch on the command line if you need it.

News and Weather

News is mostly text, so it's not a huge leap to think that there would be a number of ways to get the news on the command line. Here are two great ways to get started:

Instantnews

Instantnews Details:

Installation: sudo pip install instantnews

Run command: instantnews

Dotfile: None

163

Help: `man instantnews`

Web site: `https://github.com/shivam043/instantnews`

Instantnews retrieves all news headlines from the News API and then displays what you want to see in text. There are dozens of professional news sources, and you can choose from one or any combination of them to display on your screen. It requires you to sign up for a free API key.

Haxor-News

Haxor-News Details:

Installation: `sudo pip install haxor-news`

Run command: `hn <command>`

Dotfile: various files inside `~/.haxornewsconfig`

Help: `hn --help`

Web site: `https://github.com/donnemartin/haxor-news`

A slightly more "fun" news program that works similarly is **Haxor-News**. Haxor-News brings hacker and nerd news to the terminal, allowing you to view and filter the following without leaving your command line:

- Posts

- Post comments

- Post-linked web content

- Monthly hiring and freelancers posts

- User info

- Onion posts

Once you are in, you type various commands starting with "hn" such as `hn top` to show the top stories right now. Figure 6-22 shows an example of the output.

```
haxor> hn top
  1.   Show HN: Slim – Build 23MB micro-VM from Dockerfile, boots in seconds (github.com)
       124 points by chrisparnin 3 hours ago | 14 comments
  2.   Common Lisp: Numbers (lispcookbook.github.io)
       53 points by tosh 2 hours ago | 1 comments
  3.   My Personal Journey from MIT to GPL (drewdevault.com)
       63 points by robenkleene 1 hour ago | 20 comments
  4.   Formatting Floating Point Numbers (zverovich.net)
       116 points by matt_d 5 hours ago | 61 comments
  5.   Luna – A WYSIWYG language for data processing (luna-lang.org)
       73 points by tillulen 4 hours ago | 21 comments
  6.   Map of the World's Nuclear Power Plants (carbonbrief.org)
       45 points by ejhowell 3 hours ago | 36 comments
  7.   How the pursuit of leisure drives internet use (economist.com)
       42 points by pseudolus 2 days ago | 23 comments
  8.   Game Builder: Create 3D games with friends, no experience required (blog.google)
       393 points by sohkamyung 14 hours ago | 120 comments
  9.   I got asked LeetCode questions for a dev-ops systems engineering job today (reddit.com)
       89 points by dionmanu 2 hours ago | 102 comments
 10.   Magnesium and major depression (2011) (ncbi.nlm.nih.gov)
       150 points by known 5 hours ago | 132 comments
Tip: View the page or comments for 1 through 10 with the following command:
     hn view [#] optional: [-c] [-cr] [-cu] [-cq "regex"] [-ch] [-b] [--help]

haxor> []
```

Figure 6-22. *Haxor-News top stories*

Once you find a story that you want to read, type hn view # to
view that particular story. Figure 6-23 shows what I get after entering
"hn view 10."

```
Magnesium and major depression

George A. Eby, Karen L. Eby, and Harald Murk.

[Author Information][22]

Authors

George A. Eby,1 Karen L. Eby,1 and Harald Murk2.

Affiliations

1 George Eby Research Institute, 14909-C 2109 Paramount Avenue, Austin, Texas 78704, USA.

[moc.hcraeser-ybe-egroeg@ybe.egroeG][23]

2 Clinic of Psychiatry and Psychotherapy, University of Marburg, 35043 Marburg, Germany.

Abstract

The treatment of major depression (MD) is still a major unmet medical need in the majority of patients
. Sixty percent of cases of MD are treatment-resistant depression (TRD), showing that classical treatm
ents for MD are poorly effective to non-effective. Magnesium has been largely removed from processed f
oods, especially refined grains, in the Western world, harming the brain and causing mood disorders. M
agnesium deficiency causes N-methyl-D-aspartate (NMDA) coupled calcium channels to be biased towards o
pening which causes neuronal injury and neurological dysfunction, which we believe results in MD. Oral
 administration of Mg to animals produced antidepressant-like effects that were comparable to those of
 antidepressant drugs. Cerebral spinal fluid (CSF) Mg has been found to be low in suicidal TRD. The fi
rst report of Mg treatment for agitated depression was published in 1921 showing success in 220 out of
 250 cases. One 2008 randomized clinical trial showed that Mg was as effective as the tricyclic antide
pressant imipramine in treating MD. Intravenous and oral Mg protocols have been reported to rapidly te
rminate MD safely and without side effects. Brain Mg deficiency reduces serotonin levels, and antidepr
:█
```

Figure 6-23. *News article "Magnesium and Major Depression"*

Then hit "q" to go back to the article list and choose more.

Newsboat

Newsboat Details:

Installation: `sudo apt install newsboat`

Run command: `newsboat`

Dotfile: `~/.config/newsboat/config`

Help: `man newsboat`

Web site: `https://newsboat.org/`

Newsboat is an RSS reader. Many web sites, including most major news sources, offer an RSS feed containing their stories, so there's a huge variety of possible news sources that you can tap into. Various commands will be displayed that show how to set it up. Once you have a collection of RSS feeds installed in it, you will see something like Figure 6-24.

```
1. brian@ubuntu-612mb-nyc3-01: ~/instantnews (newsboat)
newsboat 2.11.1 - Your feeds (21 unread, 26 total)
   1 N        (5/5) Letters of Note
   2 N      (10/10) WTD
   3          (0/0) http://www.mentalfloss.com/blogs/feed
   4 N      (10/10) Schlock Mercenary
   5 N        (4/4) xkcd.com
   6 N        (5/5) PHD Comics
   7 N        (5/5) Pixelmatortutorials.net
   8 N        (5/5) Pixelmatortutorials.net (MP4)
   9 N  (1378/1378) Apple Newsroom
  10 N      (30/30) MacStories
  11 N      (48/48) Daring Fireball
  12 N      (10/10) Copyblogger
  13 N      (10/10) Writer Unboxed
  14 N        (5/5) Daily Writing Tips
  15 N      (10/10) Charlotte Rains Dixon
  16          (0/0) http://wa.emergent-publishing.com/feed/
  17 N      (10/10) Men with Pens
  18 N      (10/10) Advice to Writers
  19 N      (10/10) Inkygirl: An Illustrated Guide For Writers
  20 N        (8/8) Writing Forward
  21 N      (10/10) Mysterious Matters: Mystery Publishing Demystified
  22          (0/0) http://feeds.gawker.com/Lifehacker/full
  23          (0/0) http://podiobooks.com/index.xml
  24 N      (13/13) MakeUseOf
  25 N      (14/14) Quantum Vibe
  26          (0/0) http://feeds.feedburner.com/todoist/QCjt

q:Quit ENTER:Open n:Next Unread r:Reload R:Reload All A:Mark Read C:Mark All Read /:Search
```

Figure 6-24. *Newsbeuter/Newsboat list of feeds*

Weather

There are a great many utilities for getting weather information from the command line, so here are a few fun apps:

Finger

For the lucky people who live in a supported city, you can simply type

```
sudo apt install finger
finger city@graph.no
```

at the command line, substituting your city name for "city" in the command, and the result is something like Figure 6-25.

```
finger newyork@graph.no
```

```
brian@raspberrypi:~ $ clear
brian@raspberrypi:~ $ finger newyork@graph.no
          -= Meteogram for united_states/new_york/new_york~5128581 =-
 °C                                                              Rain
 22                    ^ ^ ^ ^ ^ ^
 21       ^^^.......        ...
 20     ^^^
 19^^^                    . . .                           ^^^
 18
 17                      ^^^^^^                     = . .
 16                    . . . = . .
 15                         = . . . . . = . .
 14                                     . . . . . . . = . .
 13
    12 13 14 15 16 17 18 19 20 21 22 23 00 01 02 03 04 05 06 07 08 09 Hour

     W  W  W NW NW NW  W NW NW  W SW SW SW SW SW SW SW SW SW SW SW SW Wind dir.
     7  8  8  8  7  7  6  5  4  3  3  3  4  4  3  4  4  3  2  3  3  3 Wind(mps)

Legend left axis:   - Sunny   ^ Scattered  = Clouded  =V= Thunder  # Fog
Legend right axis:  | Rain    ! Sleet     * Snow
[Weather forecast from yr.no, delivered by the Norwegian Meteorological Institute and the NRK.]
brian@raspberrypi:~ $
```

Figure 6-25. *Getting the weather for New York City*

Alternately, you can simply type

```
curl wttr.in/your_location
```

at the command line, substituting your city name for "your_location" in the command.

For example, if I type

```
curl wttr.in/flint
```

the output will result in something along the lines of Figure 6-26.

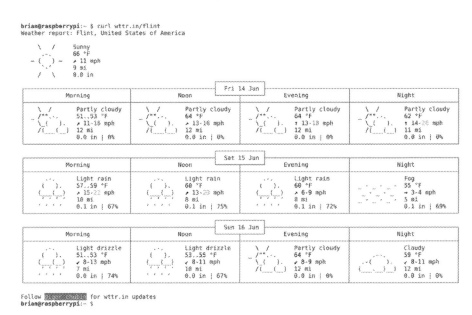

Figure 6-26. *Getting the weather for Flint, Michigan*

Ansiweather

Ansiweather Details:

Installation: `sudo apt install ansiweather`

Example run command: `ansiweather -l Flint -u imperial -f 3 -s true`

Dotfile: `~/.ansiweatherrc`

Help: `man ansiweather`

Web site: https://github.com/fcambus/ansiweather

The preceding example run command looks up the weather for Flint and reports it for 3 days, in Imperial units (i.e., not metric) along with weather symbols. As Figure 6-27 demonstrates, the preceding Ansiweather command outputs a single line with all the information on it.

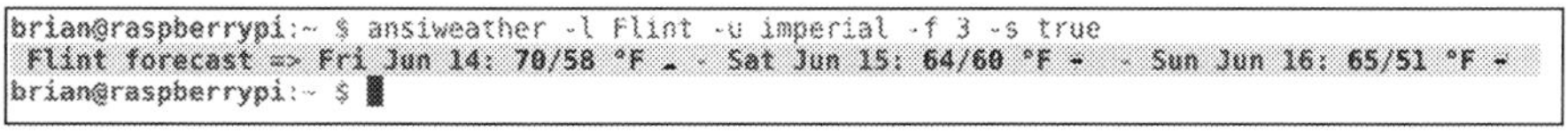

```
brian@raspberrypi:~ $ ansiweather -l Flint -u imperial -f 3 -s true
 Flint forecast => Fri Jun 14: 70/58 °F -  - Sat Jun 15: 64/60 °F -  - Sun Jun 16: 65/51 °F -
brian@raspberrypi:~ $ █
```

Figure 6-27. *Ansiweather for Flint, Michigan*

Books, Comics, and Reading

This is text mode we're dealing with now, so obviously you can read text on it. We've talked about text editors in a previous section, and those are all wonderful for simply reading text. Sometimes, however, you have a file in a non-textual format that needs to be read. Ebook formats such as EPUB, MOBI, PRC, and the like all require specialized readers; and we'll look at how to access these now.

EPUB Documents

EPUBReader Details:

Installation (type as one line):

sudo pip3 install git+https://github.com/wustho/epr.git

Run command: epr <filename.epub>

Dotfile: none

Help: epr --help

Web site: https://github.com/wustho/epr/

Generally, reading from the command line is done through a text editor such as Vim or Emacs or even Nano. Still, more and more books are being made available in ebook formats. Once installed, just type

```
epub FILENAME.epub
```

and the ebook (in EPUB format) will display on the screen. The instructions are very easy to follow.

Non-EPUB Formats

Calibre Details:

Installation: `sudo apt install calibre`

Run command: `calibre (or command in the following)`

Dotfile: set in the app through a menu

Help: `man calibre`

Web site: `https://calibre-ebook.com/`

Other ebook formats, such as .mobi, .azw, and .prc, will need to be converted to .epub or text format before use. The most common way to do this from within a graphical user interface is with the app **Calibre**. Since we're talking about command-line tools here, most of Calibre's features won't be available, but Calibre *does* come with several powerful command-line tools.

Once you have Calibre installed, you can use its graphic interface if you choose (as in Figure 6-28), but if you want to do it all from the command line, check out the command-line tools installed alongside Calibre.

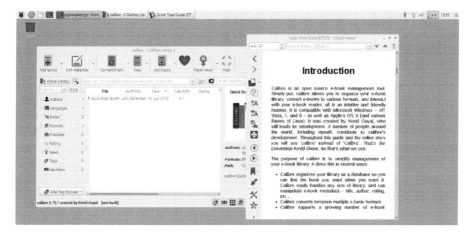

Figure 6-28. *Calibre on the desktop*

Documented commands:

- calibre
- calibre-customize
- calibre-debug
- calibre-server
- calibre-smtp
- calibredb
- ebook-convert
- ebook-edit
- ebook-meta
- ebook-polish
- ebook-viewer
- fetch-ebook-metadata
- lrf2lrs

- lrfviewer

- lrs2lrf

- web2disk

The list and associated instructions can be found at https://manual.calibre-ebook.com/generated/en/cli-index.html.

Probably the most useful one is ebook-convert. If, for example, you have an ebook file in .mobi format and you want to change it to .epub format, just type

```
ebook-convert myfile.mobi myfile.epub -h
```

It's really fast, and the output looks perfect. Then you can just use the EPUB reader to read the file.

Task Management

There are many command-line tools for calendaring, scheduling, and task management. Here are my favorites:

Cal

From way back in the early days of the original Unix systems, there is the ancient cal command. It displays a monthly calendar with today's date highlighted. I can't begin to tell how many times I've used this over the years. Other than displaying the month, it doesn't *do* anything special, but it's still incredibly convenient.

It's part of the operating system, so you don't need to install anything. Just type

```
cal
```

Calcurse

Calcurse Details:

Installation: `sudo apt install calcurse`

Run command: `calcurse`

Dotfile: Various files in `~/.calcurse/`

Help: `man calcurse`

Web site: `https://calcurse.org/`

Calcurse is a visual, text-based calendar, scheduler, and to-do manager for the command line. It has commands listed along the bottom two lines, much like the Nano editor, and additional commands can be had by hitting the "o" key. It allows customizations of colors, the layout of the three main window panes, and a few other things that you can select. If you aren't worried about syncing between your computer and other devices, this is probably the nicest way to go. There's a nice screenshot in Figure 6-29.

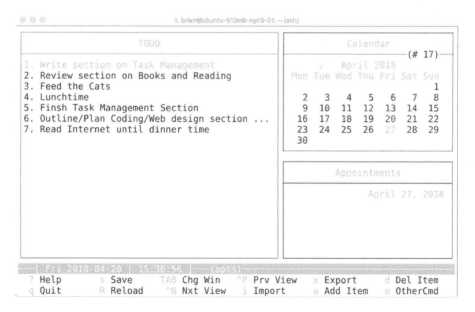

Figure 6-29. *Calcurse*

173

Todo.txt

If you are concerned about syncing your appointments and tasks between devices, this process is more complex than Calcurse, but allows for use on any device. The concept is simple: A group of users have gotten together and created a standardized text file format that can contain all your to-do lists and appointments. Then you use a file-syncing system like Dropbox to make that file available to your computer, phone, tablet, and whatever other devices you use. It's easy to set this system up, it's reliable, and it's surprisingly flexible.

If what I've just described is something that appeals to you, then by all means go for it right now and design your own methodology and system. Put a todo.txt file in your Dropbox on your phone and set your computer to access that file. You're all set!

Or you can use a system already available that does all this. There's a whole online community that has built up around this concept, and they've come up with what they believe is a "standard" for todo.txt files. The home page for the organizations is at

```
http://todotxt.org
```

and the specific "rules" they have set up are at

```
https://github.com/todotxt/todo.txt.
```

You might ask, "Why use such a complicated set of rules for simply managing a to-do list in a text file?" The answer is that if you use their standardized format, then you can take advantage of the various apps that have been created to support the format. If you don't care about these apps, then you *could* just do it any way you want, managing your files with a text editor.

There is todo.txt-cli at

```
https://github.com/todotxt/todo.txt-cli/releases
```

as well as other apps that do the same thing. This idea especially appeals when you realize there are phone apps that work with these files. My favorite for the iPhone is SwiftoDo, found at `http://swiftodoapp.com/`. Figure 6-30 shows the app. Text files and command lines are great on a full-sized computer, but on a little phone, specialized apps really are easier to deal with than trying to edit a text file with a general writing app.

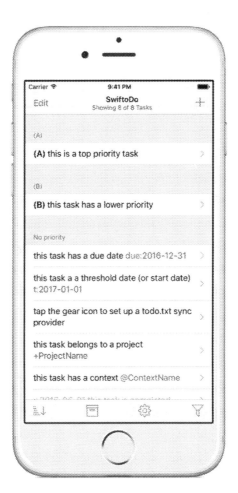

Figure 6-30. *SwiftoDo for iPhone*

Coding/Programming/Web Design

The options and availability of Linux-based programming and coding tools are nearly unlimited. Almost every computer language compiler is available as a command-line tool, and, under the surface, even most GUI programming tools simply run a command-line tool in the background. The best way to get into coding is to choose a text editor program such as Vim, Emacs, or something of that sort and then start looking at the various syntax tools and programming-specific plug-ins.

All the major text editors are used heavily by developers, mostly due to their customizability, plug-in capability, and speed. Which editor you choose is largely a matter of taste and how much effort you want to put into learning it; it's completely possible to use nothing more than Nano to type in code and then compile it on the command line using the language of your choice, but most coders are going to want something more and will quickly advance into Emacs or Vim (although there are other choices out there that are excellent as well). There's no way I can even begin to scratch the surface of how to use these advanced editors in the development world, so I won't. Just keep in mind that coding in text mode is just as capable, if not more, as working in a GUI environment.

One coding tool that has exploded in the past few years is *Git*. Git is a free and open source distributed *version control system* designed to handle everything from small to very large projects with speed and efficiency. Git is easy to learn and has a tiny footprint with lightning-fast performance. It ties in with `Github.com`, the online repository and home of most of today's open source projects. The command-line version of Git is available at `https://git-scm.com` and can be installed as either a command-line version or GUI tool. Once you make some changes to a source file (whatever kind, from C++ to HTML to Prose Text), you commit changes to a repository, and then if you decide to branch off or restore from a previous version at a later time, you can. It's tremendously useful for keeping multiple versions of files, collaboration, and, of course, bug fixes.

Web Apps and Services

Installing command-line software isn't the only option to get things done anymore. There are also countless web applications available over the Internet for free or for a subscription fee. Some people survive just fine using nothing but a Chromebook as their primary computer, and, until recently, those machines used nothing but web applications, and we're looking at them in this book as almost an afterthought. Many advanced web sites depend heavily on JavaScript and other scripting languages that do not work well (or at all) from a text-based browser, but some work well in text mode.

There are command-line tools to access many web-based services. **Todoist** is one very popular to-do list manager that works great on most mobile devices, and there is at least one good command-line interface for it. The **todo.txt** system is another system that works to sync between mobile/GUI and text.

This book isn't going to focus too heavily on web apps, as I cover them extensively in my other book, *Going Chromebook: Living Life in the Cloud*, and really only intend to cover text-mode specific tools here. Just keep in mind that if you can't find a tool you need, there may be a tool on the Web for your needs.

Using Command-Line Tools with the GUI

Sometimes the best tool for a job is not the one you *want* to be using. Sometimes, the GUI really is the more efficient way to do things. Drawing and video work are two good examples, as is image-intensive web development. Most heavily visual game programming requires a GUI. Plus, some modern tools *only* work under a windowing system, not even making their features available from the command line. Sometimes you *need* a GUI to get things done.

The days of dumb terminals and text-based teletype machines are long past us. Nostalgia and minimalism are enjoyable, but there is a reason that computers have moved past those things. If you're running a command-line tool on a server with SSH, then you can do a lot of powerful things that way, but if you add that power alongside the best tools that a GUI system can offer, wouldn't that be better still? Sometimes, you may find yourself following a ten-step process to get something done that you could be using a different tool for and doing it in a single step.

My point is that now that you've learned how you can do just about everything in text mode, it's time to select what works best for you and use those tools alongside your desktop software. If you've been running a command line from within a terminal window on a Raspbian machine, or SSH-ing into your Pi from a Mac, then you're already doing this. Terminator or Terminal on Linux is the same thing; you're running a terminal screen from within a GUI. That's not "cheating"; that's the smart way to do it.

For example, writing a book is one task that needs both ways of working to finish a project. Go ahead and write that book in LaTeX or Markdown using Vim. Use the command-line version of Git to manage your versions. Compile it into a PDF with Pandoc. But then use some graphic app such as Okular to view the resulting PDF. This is called "using the right tool for the right job" and is the most efficient way to get the project done. If you can't find a command-line PDF viewer that you enjoy using, then don't do it that way. It's all about what gets things done in the most efficient and enjoyable manner. It's OK to get hung up in your work; just don't get bogged down by the tools.

Learn how to cut and paste from the terminal window into a graphical window. Learn how to copy files from your home directory onto the desktop of the graphical desktop. Sometimes it's easier to use Ranger to browse the file system than it is to use the File Manager, and sometimes the opposite is true.

Just off the top of my head, I've provided two lists of tasks that I believe are better suited for one method or the other (Table 6-1). You can do all these things from one "side" or the other; these are just what I find preferable. Your opinion is free to vary.

Table 6-1. *Command Line vs. GUI*

Better from the Command Line	Better in a Graphical Environment
Mutt for email	PDF and comic reading
Text editing using Vim or Emacs	Complex desktop publishing layouts
Ranger/MC for file operations	Drawing and graphic creation
Music and playlist creation	Most games
File backups, large-scale file transfers, and big downloads	Web browsing

My point here is that the command line doesn't have to be a "lifestyle." It's one more tool in your arsenal of computer power. By learning the command line and some of the more useful tools, you can gain faster and more powerful ways to do things in a more customizable environment, often using less-powerful equipment. This whole concept is meant to be fun, not a prison sentence.

Conclusion

There are some tasks, like video and audio editing, that really demand the use of graphic mode and a mouse. That said, most tasks work just fine from the command line. They may not have all the pretty bells and whistles that accompany most desktop apps, but they often are far more configurable and easier to access and have extremely advanced automation possibilities. It's just a matter of figuring out how they work without all the easy menus that a GUI offers.

In the next chapter, we'll look at advanced topics and things that didn't fit elsewhere. We've discussed Markdown and LaTeX, and we'll do a quick introduction to those tools and then look at customizing your command-line apps with dotfiles and configuration files. We'll look at some additional resources you can find online.

Lastly, we look at some projects you can use a *spare* Raspberry Pi for that require a dedicated machine. I've found that the RPi are so cheap, you tend to buy a new one every time they have a significant upgrade. I recently looked, and I have five of them lying around!

CHAPTER 7

Advanced Topics

The topics covered in this chapter are valuable options to consider when working from either the command line or GUI—or both in many cases.

First, we talk about Markdown and LaTeX, two "languages" for describing text that allows for easier conversion to other formats. Markdown can be learned in under half an hour, while LaTeX is much more complex but also much more flexible. Generally speaking, if you are writing for EPUB or HTML for web-based publishing, I would recommend learning Markdown. If you are writing for PDF or print publishing, I'd look at LaTeX, but there is a lot of crossover between the two.

Second, we look at what are generally called "dotfiles." I've mentioned repeatedly that text apps are extremely customizable, but we haven't really delved into it. The dotfiles are where configuration information about each app is stored; and things like key mappings, color schemes, plug-ins, and most other customizations are accomplished by editing these files.

Third, I walk you through my dotfile for the Vim editor. I am by no means a master of Vim, but I have done some basic customizations that may appeal to a non-programmer. I'll walk you through this file step by step as an example to show what kind of things *can* be done.

We then look at using your Raspberry Pi as an emulator of other systems. The Pi runs Linux, but inside that we can run MS-DOS apps, Nintendo games, and even old coin-op arcade games.

Finally, I have included a list of links as "additional resources" for further research as well as some ideas for what to do with the "extra" Raspberry Pi computers you're likely to acquire as your interest grows.

© Brian Schell 2019
B. Schell, *Computing with the Raspberry Pi*, https://doi.org/10.1007/978-1-4842-5293-2_7

Markdown and LaTeX

In the GUI world, word processors are kings of document creation. Microsoft Word, Apple Pages, even Google Docs make document creation visual and easy. On the other hand, if you've ever gotten lost in a tangle of indentions and missing bullet points in Word, then you know how frustrating those visual formats can be. Many writers choose to work with a text editor instead of a word processor. Working with text is a mixed blessing. You have total control over every aspect of your words and data, but it comes at the cost of a higher learning curve. That sounds familiar by now, doesn't it?

I mentioned **WordGrinder** back in the "Writing Tools" section. It's the closest thing to a "word processor" I know of for a text-only system. It allows you to do boldface, underlining, and a few other formatting things; but it's not anywhere near as robust or powerful as any of the GUI word processors. It is reliable and easy to learn; it may be enough for you.

On the other hand, if you do a lot of writing, or require more precise formatting, there are two very popular systems of *describing* your text formatting: **Markdown** and **LaTeX**. Which of these you decide to learn depends on the kind of writing you do as well as what kind of output you desire.

I have included two examples in the following, one of Markdown and the other of LaTeX, and neither of them includes any explanation. As you can see from these two examples, Markdown is relatively easy to read, even for someone who doesn't actually know that the material they are looking at is Markdown. It's easy to follow and easy to learn; usually it's just the addition of certain punctuation characters to plain text, like # for various headings, ** for bold and * for italic, and []() for links and graphics. It's much easier to learn than HTML, but allows for very similar output. In fact, Markdown was originally created to easily convert a text document into HTML for posting to a blog, but it's useful for most forms of online writing.

LaTeX, on the other hand, is scattered with a huge number of tags and brackets and generally has more "overhead." That said, the overhead and complexity allow essentially unlimited flexibility with printed layouts—more books have been typeset with LaTeX than any other method since computers first started being used in printing.

Of course, both Markdown and LaTeX are simply "markup languages" that describe the text, much in the same way HTML does. Both text languages are simply text files that are edited using the text editor of your choice—Vim or Emacs; or even Nano could be used. Of course, since they are simply text files, they are, by definition, completely cross-platform. If you decide to go back to Windows, Mac, or Linux someday, you can take all these files with you as the same tools are available for those platforms as well. The same goes with iOS, Android, decades-old mainframes, and every computer that hasn't been invented yet.

Text files are never going to "go away" or change significantly enough that it can't be read by something. The same cannot be said for word processing formats—think of files saved in Apple Works, Microsoft Works, or even early versions of Apple Pages, none of which can be read in modern word processing software. Those files have essentially become unreadable.

The process of using the text languages is quite simple. You just type in the "code" as shown in the following using your favorite text editor. Remember the *.md* or *.tex* file that you write is not the final document; it will be compiled using an app like *Pandoc* or *LaTeX* to create an output file in the format that you need: *.docx*, *.pdf*, *.odt*, or whatever you want. There are dozens of output formats that you can use.

Markdown

If you're writing for the Web or for ebooks, you probably should take a look at Markdown. It easily converts to HTML and EPUB formats, and it's extremely easy to learn. You can probably pick up the basics by watching a 10-minute YouTube video!

Heading
=======

Sub-heading

Paragraphs are separated by a blank line.

Two spaces at the end of
a line leave a line break.

Text attributes *italic*, **bold**, `monospace`.

Horizontal rule:

Bullet list:

* apples
* oranges
* pears

Numbered list:

1. wash
2. rinse
3. repeat

A [link](http://example.com).

![Image](Image_icon.png)

Pandoc

To convert the preceding Markdown text into a more useful final format, I would have to recommend **Pandoc**. It can convert nearly any format to any other format. Type

```
sudo apt install pandoc
```

to install it. To use it, you type something like the following:

```
pandoc -f markdown -t docx example.md -o example.docx
```

This will take the file *example.md* (.md indicates that it's a markdown file) and convert it to *example.docx* (a Microsoft Word file). Note the various flags and arguments for the command:

`pandoc`	The main command
`-f markdown`	**From** the markdown format
`-t docx`	**To** the docx format
`example.md`	Source file (ends in md for markdown)
`-o`	**Output**
`example.docx`	Output file (ends in docx for Word document)

Pandoc is an immensely powerful conversion utility, and it supports literally dozens of different input and output formats.

You can read the man page by typing man pandoc and paging through it all, or for something a little more reader-friendly, try the web site at https://pandoc.org/MANUAL.html.

LaTeX

If you are writing with paper in mind, printouts or books or reports (or PDFs), you may want to look into LaTeX. LaTeX is a high-quality typesetting system; it includes features designed for the production of technical and scientific documentation. LaTeX is the de facto standard for the communication and publication of scientific and mathematical documents. It was designed to be run on the mini-computers of the 1970s, so the Pi is more than powerful enough to handle any LaTeX project you can come up with.

```latex
\documentclass{article}
\usepackage{amsmath}
\title{\LaTeX}
\begin{document}
\maketitle
\LaTeX{} is a document preparation system for the \TeX{}
typesetting program. It offers programmable desktop publishing
features and extensive facilities for automating most aspects
of typesetting and desktop publishing, including numbering
and  cross-referencing, tables and figures, page layout,
bibliographies, and much more. \LaTeX{} was originally written
in 1984 by Leslie Lamport and has become the  dominant method
for using \TeX; few people write in plain \TeX{} anymore.
The current version is \LaTeXe.
% This is a comment, not shown in final output.
% The following shows typesetting  power of LaTeX:
\begin{align}
E_0 &= mc^2 \\
E &= \frac{mc^2}{\sqrt{1-\frac{v^2}{c^2}}}
\end{align}
\end{document}
```

To install the compiler for LaTeX, type the following. Keep in mind that Tex Live is a *very* large download and install, so make sure you have at least 2GB of disk space on your SD card or hard drive before installing this:

```
sudo apt update
sudo apt install texlive-full
sudo apt install texworks
```

If you don't think you'll need the very advanced tools offered within the texlive-full package, you can substitute the following in place of the third line above:

```
sudo apt install texlive
```

Also, if you don't have a particularly favorite text editor, you can install Texmaker, an editor specially designed for working with LaTeX:

```
sudo apt install texmaker
```

There was a brief description of Texmaker back in Chapter 4. If you'd prefer a much more graphical option, there are completely online, cloud-based LaTeX editors. Check out Overleaf.com for what is easily the best example. It works great on the Chromium browser from the Pi as well, and you don't need to install anything to make it work. It even stores your writing in the cloud, so you don't have to worry about losing anything.

Customization with Dotfiles

Throughout the book, I've mentioned over and over just how *customizable* everything is, but I haven't touched on how to do any of that customization. Some text-based apps have drop-down menus and settings that are adjusted just like the settings in a graphically based app. If that's the case, then you probably know how to do that already.

The more powerful method is by editing "dotfiles." These are files containing settings, variables, and fields that you can change with a text editor like Vim, Emacs, or even Nano. The files are usually named after the app itself, only they start with a period (hence "dotfiles"), and sometimes they have "rc" added at the end. Some examples might be

.vimrc

.emacs

.muttrc

.tmux.config

.config

Note   The following applies to any variety of Linux. Check the documentation for specific apps to see where the configuration files are stored and how to access them.

To see what I'm talking about, go to your home directory in the terminal and do a full directory list:

```
cd ~
ls -la
```

You may need to scroll up and down to see everything, but there are going to be a number of files that start with a period. These files can be edited, changed, and then saved to alter permanent settings for the apps. Note that dotfiles are "invisible" to the basic ls command, so you must use the -la switch to see them. They may also be hidden if you use Ranger or Midnight Commander to view the directory listing.

Every app has different rules and settings, and there's no way I can explain them all (even if I understood them all). The best way to go about this is to use an app in its default state, and then as soon as you find yourself thinking "I wonder if there's a better way to ..." or "I wish this worked differently," then go online (or check the man file) and do a search for the app's configuration options. There's a very good chance there is a setting or a plug-in that does exactly what you need. Most apps are surprisingly flexible, but you will find that most commend-line/text-mode apps don't have extensive built-in menus.

As an example, I use the Vim text editor a lot, and I have modified its configuration file quite a bit. In the next section, I will go over my dotfile for Vim. Most other apps work in similar ways.

My .vimrc File

The Vim app is mostly configured through a file called *.vimrc*. The **.vimrc** file is located in your HOME directory. To edit it, type

```
nano ~/.vimrc
```

If you don't already have a .vimrc file, this will create one for you.

When the Vim application is started, it scans the home directory and looks for this file. If it isn't there, Vim runs under its own generic defaults, but if it does exist, it reads the files and changes Vim's behavior according to what's in the configuration file. Here's mine (the line numbers are for your reference; the real file doesn't have those):

```
01 filetype off
02 set encoding=utf-8
03
04 execute pathogen#infect()
05 execute pathogen#helptags()
06 let g:airline_theme='jellybeans'
07
08 filetype plugin indent on
09 :let mapleader = ","
10
11 nnoremap j gj
```

```
12 nnoremap k gk
13 vnoremap j gj
14 vnoremap k gk
15 nnoremap <Down> gj
16 nnoremap <Up> gk
17 vnoremap <Down> gj
18 vnoremap <Up> gk
19 inoremap <Down> <C-o>gj
20 inoremap <Up> <C-o>gk
21
22 " Nerdtree start and toggle ,-n and ,-m
23 :map <Leader>n  <Esc>:NERDTree<CR>
24 :map <Leader>m  <Esc>:NERDTreeToggle<CR>
25
26 "Latex compile and preview key bindings
27 :map <Leader>u  <Esc>:! pdflatex "%"
28 :map <Leader>i  <Esc>:! evince "%:t:r.pdf" &
29
30 " Spell check toggle
31 :map <F6> :setlocal spell! spelllang=en_us<CR>
32
33 colorscheme slate
34 set nocompatible
35 set nonumber
36 set guioptions-=L
37 set guioptions-=T
38 set ruler
39 set undolevels=1000
40 :set wrap linebreak nolist
41
42 :set display+=lastline
43 :abbreviate img ![](.jpg)
```

That looks like a lot of really technical stuff, but this is actually very short by many Vim enthusiasts' standards. Now, I'll go through this line by line and explain what's going on here.

- **Line 1:** *Filetype* tells Vim to detect what kind of file is being loaded and use syntax highlighting for that kind of file. I am not a coder, so I don't need syntax highlighting, so I turned that off.

- **Line 2:** *UTF-8* is a standard character encoding type that is used for most print and ebooks. It's also all I ever use. Settings like this, where you want to set it once and never mess with it again, are prime candidates for a change in the configuration file.

- **Lines 4 and 5:** *Pathogen* is a "plug-in manager." Vim allows extensions and plug-ins that do things not built in to the base Vim system. Pathogen takes care of loading and running the plug-in scripts for me.

- **Line 6:** *Airline* is a replacement for the plain status line at the bottom of the screen in Vim. Mine has a nice blue color with different information than what Vim provides by default. It's not really a necessity, but I like how it looks. Mine uses the theme "Jellybeans," which is set here.

- **Line 8:** Turns plug-ins and indentation on.

- **Line 9:** Vim has a thing called a "leader key" which allows you to define keyboard combinations that do just about anything you can imagine. I have my leader key set to the comma key. That means I can hit *comma-n,* and something will happen. If I hit *comma-m*, something else can happen, and so on. It's a lot like hitting the Ctrl or Alt key along with something else, but Vim has so much going on that most of the Ctrl and Alt combinations have already been taken. The leader key combinations are "all mine." We'll define these specific keys later in the file.

- **Lines 11–20:** Vim is a programmer's editor, but I mostly write text files. I don't like the way Vim moves up or down an entire paragraph when I hit the up or down arrow keys. I am used to the way regular word processors use the arrow keys, so here I have "remapped" the keys to move the way I want. In line 11, I have remapped the "j" key to use the action normally associated with the keys "gj." Line 15 does the same thing for the down arrow key. The vnoremap, nnoremap, and inoremap do the same things, but apply the changes to different modes. It's complicated, but your takeaway here is that you can remap any key on the keyboard to do anything you want. (Vim purists are now shaking their heads at this abomination, wondering why I don't just use the default movement keys). Vim is a really old application; it was literally designed before many keyboards had arrow keys on them; so the default movement are the H, J, K, and L keys.

- **Line 22:** This is a comment. It doesn't do anything.

- **Line 23:** Here's where things start to happen. This line maps the leader key I mentioned earlier with the "n" key. When I hit comma-n, the plug-in NERDTree runs. NERDTree is a file-browsing plug-in used to select and load files from a menu.

- **Line 24:** Maps the comma-m combination to make the NERDTree window go away. I can use comma-n to select and load a file and then hit comma-m to make the file selector go away.

- **Line 26:** Another comment.

- **Line 27:** Maps COMMA-U to compile the text file on the screen to a PDF using PDFLATEX. If I'm writing a LaTeX file, this will do all the compiling for me, so I don't have to remember or type the command line that normally is needed to compile a file.

- **Line 28:** Maps COMMA-I to load the Evince PDF viewer and preview the file created when I hit COMMA-U.

- **Line 31:** Maps the F6 function key to turn spell-check on or off.

- **Line 33:** There are numerous built-in color schemes you can use, or you can install your own. I use the built-in theme called "slate."

- **Line 34:** Has something to do with compatibility with the much older VI program. I don't need this compatibility, so I turn it off.

- **Line 35:** Turns line numbering off. Again, I write prose text, not code, so I don't especially care about line numbering. Note that the line you are currently on still shows in the status bar at the bottom of the screen.

- **Line 36:** In GUI mode, this removes the left-hand scroll bar.

- **Line 37:** In GUI mode, this removes the tool bar at the top of the screen.

- **Line 38:** Set ruler allows Vim to know and display on the status line which column your cursor is in.

- **Line 39:** Set the number of Undo levels.

- **Line 40:** This makes it so Vim will break a line at spaces or punctuation, but not in the middle of a word. Otherwise, Vim allows a line to go on for a very long time without wrapping to the screen.

- **Line 42:** For some reason, Vim does strange things to the lowest line of the screen. This line fixes that.

- **Line 43:** If you've ever used a tool like **TextExpander**, you'll like this. This line fixes it so that whenever I type the characters img, it automatically expands that text into the string . That's an empty placeholder for an image file when writing in Markdown. I never remember the specific characters involved, and because of this line, I don't have to. When I want to insert an image, I type img, and those characters pop up. Then I go back in and fill in the description and filename. You can set up any unique string of characters to expand into anything you want this way. For space reasons, I've only included this one abbreviation here, but it's not uncommon to have dozens of them.

- Again, a serious Vim user will customize their .vimrc file to the point where they quite simply have thousands of lines of customizations.

How did I learn to do all this? I tried using the "vanilla" Vim program, and when I hit something I didn't like, I Googled until I found the configuration commands. When you find a page that explains some modification you like, often it will link to related customizations that you can do, and then you're down a rabbit hole of crazy modifications. It's actually fun adding some powerful new function to what is otherwise such a "plain" app.

Mastering and squeezing out every last drop of power and performance out of these tools is a serious hobby for some people, and they love to write about their exploits online. At the very least, you should experiment with changing the color scheme and turning on spell-check—those are easy commands to start with. Then build things up one step at a time. My advice is also to *not* copy anyone else's configuration files—not even mine. Make up your own as your needs grow.

My .tmux.conf File

For a second, less complex example, let's look at the configuration file for Tmux, the terminal multiplexer app. The app is configured through a file called *.tmux.conf*. To edit this, type

```
nano ~/.tmux.conf
```

And if you don't already have this file, Nano will create a blank one for you. Here's what I have:

```
source-file "${HOME}/.tmux-themepack/powerline/double.blue.
tmuxtheme"
# split pane using | and -
Bind | split-window -h
Bind - split-window -v
```

Obviously, this is much shorter than the Vim configuration file; not everything is super complicated.

The first line loads a color theme for the status line that displays at the bottom of the Tmux screen. Normally, Tmux shows a plain green status line, but this one has a nice blue color and some graphic dividers. It doesn't really *do* anything useful, but I like the way it looks.

The second line is a comment, explaining the next two lines.

Line 3 "binds" the | key to the command that splits the window horizontally. The | key looks to me like the vertical slice that cuts the window in half, so I think that's easier to remember than the default key for this action.

Line 4 does the same thing, mapping the – key to the vertical split. The hyphen goes from right to left, which looks to me like the line that goes across the screen in the vertical split. I'm a bit of a visual thinker, so these two keys are just easier to remember than the default keys " and %.

So that's my .tmux.conf file. Just about every application you can find has something similar to this, although usually not so elaborate or complex as the Vim example.

If you don't see a dotfile in your root directory, look inside the ~/**.config** subdirectory; sometimes they hide them in there. If it doesn't exist in either ~/.config or your /home directory, check the documentation for the software—it almost certainly has *some method* of making permanent customizations; it's just a matter of finding the file location. It's also a very good idea to keep backups of all your customized dotfiles. That way, if you set up another machine, those files are easily available, and also if you mess something up, you can go back to the previous working version. I know many Linux users who keep all their dotfiles in a Github.org repository, a project outside the scope of this book.

This may seem at first to be unnecessarily complex. Surely, it would be easier to select options from a menu. Well, that's true if the choices are limited to what the creators of the program thought to include. Apps like Vim and Tmux allow an *unlimited* variety of plug-ins and features that border on the ridiculous. There's no way the Vim programmers would have thought to include everything, nor would they want to. Many plug-ins are *very* special purpose. By using completely open text files for configuration settings, pretty much anything goes as far as what can be created. Yes, it's more complicated, but it's *infinitely* expandable.

Other Distributions of Linux

We saw from the very beginning that there was more than one Linux distribution available for the Raspberry Pi, and we started off talking about Raspbian and Ubuntu MATE. There are others available as well, and you can try them out as you see fit by following the same process we did in the beginning: download an image file, write it to SD card (or hard drive) using Etcher, and then configure the operating system.

Some of the most popular distributions that are compatible with the Raspberry Pi include the following:

- **Raspbian** is the default Raspberry Pi operating system, created and maintained by the Raspberry Pi Foundation

  (www.raspberrypi.org/downloads/raspbian/).

- **Ubuntu MATE** is one version of Ubuntu with a complete desktop and major apps. For the most part, MATE runs slower than Raspbian, but it's much more full featured and often friendlier to use

  (https://ubuntu-mate.org/raspberry-pi/).

- **Kali Linux** is big with white-hat hackers and security testers. It doesn't come with the usual games and business apps, but it does focus heavily on security testing

  (www.kali.org/).

- **CentOS** is the community edition of the Red Hat Enterprise Linux distribution, and each new version is guaranteed to be supported for 10 years

  (www.centos.org/).

- **RISC OS** is very different from the others in that it's **not** based on Linux in any way. It's very fast and very small, but it does things in unusual ways compared to Linux systems

  (`www.riscosopen.org`).

- **RASPBSD** is a version of FreeBSD for the Pi. FreeBSD also isn't Linux, but a full version of Unix, the OS that Linux was based upon

  (`www.raspbsd.org/`).

- **Windows IoT Core and Ubuntu Core** are two specialized versions of the respective operating systems that are not full desktop environments, but are "core" systems, scaled down to take advantage of the Pi's cheap hardware to create Internet-connected "Internet of Things" devices

  (`https://docs.microsoft.com/en-us/windows/iot-core/downloads`

  `https://ubuntu.com/download/iot/raspberry-pi-2-3-core`).

- **Pi MusicBox** turns your Pi into a jukebox, loading your music from local and networked storage drives as well as many streaming sources like Spotify and Google Play Music

  (`www.pimusicbox.com/`).

- **LibreELEC** is designed to run the Kodi media center. You connect it to your TV/monitor and a hard drive full of videos and music, and it turns your TV into a *very* smart TV

  (`https://libreelec.tv/downloads/`).

- **OpenMediaVault** turns your Raspberry Pi into the brains of a Network-Attached Storage (NAS). Just add one or more large hard drives, and plug the Pi into your network, and you've got a smart NAS

  (www.openmediavault.org).

- **RetroPie** is a "retro" video game emulation system. We'll talk more about emulators in the next section, but this distribution includes apps that emulate dozens of older computers

  (https://retropie.org.uk/).

DOSBox and Emulation Software

Still, there *are* other possibilities. With a "full power" computer, virtual computing and emulators are a major area of hobbyist interest. Can you run emulators on the Raspberry Pi? Of course you can! Emulating old video game systems is one of the most common hobby uses of the Pi.

One of the most popular and thoroughly debugged emulators is called DOSBox. It allows you to run software created for MS-DOS from the 1980s and 1990s and run it right on your Raspberry Pi. This could be once-popular software such as WordPerfect 5.1, Lotus 1-2-3, Wildcat! BBS, or other powerful software. On the other hand, it could also be some of the thousands of great games written before Windows 95 took over the PC world: Wing Commander, M.U.L.E., Zork, Tetris, and a bunch more. These games don't have to be lost to time; you can run them on your Raspberry Pi right now.

To get started, download DOSBox:

```
sudo apt install dosbox
```

Run it with `dosbox`.

Figure 7-1 shows the output of the MS-DOS `dir` command.

```
DOSBox 0.74-2, Cpu speed:    3...ameskip 0, Program:  DOSBOX
Z:\>mem

       632 Kb free conventional memory
        63 Kb free upper memory in 1 blocks (largest UMB 63 Kb)
     15168 Kb free extended memory
     15168 Kb free expanded memory

Z:\>dir
Directory of Z:\.
COMMAND  COM                 20 01-10-2002 12:34
AUTOEXEC BAT                 32 01-10-2002 12:34
KEYB     COM                 20 01-10-2002 12:34
IMGMOUNT COM                 20 01-10-2002 12:34
BOOT     COM                 20 01-10-2002 12:34
INTRO    COM                 20 01-10-2002 12:34
RESCAN   COM                 20 01-10-2002 12:34
LOADFIX  COM                 20 01-10-2002 12:34
MEM      COM                 20 01-10-2002 12:34
MOUNT    COM                 20 01-10-2002 12:34
MIXER    COM                 20 01-10-2002 12:34
CONFIG   COM                 20 01-10-2002 12:34
    12 File(s)              252 Bytes.
     0 Dir(s)                 0 Bytes free.

Z:\>
```

Figure 7-1. *DOSBox DOS prompt*

If you are familiar with MS-DOS, most all commands will work. Copy files, delete files, directory listings—it's all here. The first step in running a game or app is to "map" a directory in your home folder to the C: drive in "DOS." This makes it appear to DOS that you have these apps installed on your main DOS hard drive.

For example, if you have recently downloaded a collection of games that are stored in ~/Downloads/DOS, you would mount this folder as your C: drive in DOS:

```
mount c ~/Downloads/DOS
```

Now if you type

```
dir c
```

you should now see the contents of the DOS folder on your Linux drive. Next, you would change the active directory to one with a specific game in it with the cd command.

```
cd warcra~1
```

takes me into the "Warcraft" directory. Then you can type dir to see all the files in the folder and find the .exe file, which is *usually* an executable file in DOS. For the game I am trying to run, the executable file is called war.exe. Type

```
war
```

and the game will not only start, but it will work surprisingly well. Figure 7-2 shows a screenshot.

DOSBox is also somewhat customizable using dotfiles. The configuration for it can be accessed by typing

```
nano ~/.dosbox/dosbox-0.74-2.conf
```

Note that this could be different if you have a newer version of the app. Two useful things to change in this file are as follows:

1) You can set it to automatically mount the C: drive as we did earlier. Just type in the "mount" command in the configuration file

   ```
   mount c ~/Downloads/DOS
   ```

   or whatever location you use for your DOS apps.

2) Near the top of the file is a line fullscreen=false. If you change this to fullscreen=true and then save the file, DOSBox will start opening in full-screen mode, which looks much better than the tiny window you'll get otherwise.

This section isn't meant to be a DOS emulator tutorial so much as it is an example of one type of emulator that is available to you. There are similar emulators available for Nintendo, Game Boy, Genesis, and most other older arcade and console games.

All the details, notes, and help files can be found at the DOSBox web site, `http://dosbox.com`, shown in Figure 7-2.

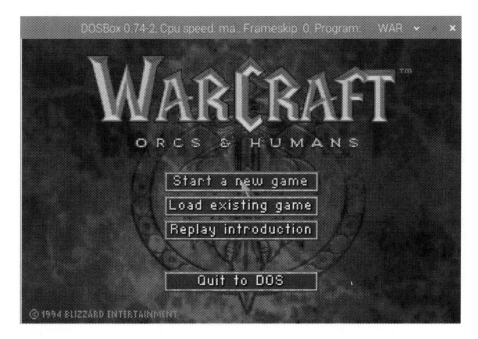

Figure 7-2. *The DOS Game Warcraft from 1994*

RetroPie

And if running old PC games isn't enough to entertain you, you might want to look into trying a specialized emulation distribution like RetroPie. RetroPie, once installed, will boot your Pi into a menu of old computers, consoles, and videogame machines and then allow you to load games from those systems. There are emulators included for dozens of systems such as follows:

3do	Neo Geo
Amiga	Neo Geo Pocket
Amstrad CPC	Neo Geo Pocket Color
Apple II	Oric-1/Atmos
Atari 2600	PC
Atari 5200 and 8-bit series	PC Engine/TurboGrafx-16
Atari 7800	PC-FX
Atari Jaguar	PSP
Atari Lynx	Nintendo DS
Atari ST/STE/TT/Falcon	Nintendo NES
CoCo	PlayStation 1
Colecovision	PlayStation 2
Commodore 64	ResidualVM
Daphne	SAM Coupé
Dragon 32	Saturn
Dreamcast	ScummVM
FinalBurn Alpha	Sega 32X
GameCube	Sega CD
Game & Watch	Sega SG-1000
Game Gear	Super Nintendo
Game Boy	TI-99/4A
Game Boy Color	TRS-80
Game Boy Advance	Vectrex
Intellivision	Videopac/Odyssey2
Macintosh	Virtual Boy
MAME	Wii
Master System	WonderSwan
Mega Drive/Genesis	WonderSwan Color
MESS	Zmachine
MSX	ZX Spectrum
Nintendo 64	

Additional Resources

- Using the Linux command line (pdf book)

  `http://linuxcommand.org/tlcl.php`

- Plaintext Productivity

  `http://plaintext-productivity.net/`

- Inconsolation: Adventures with lightweight and minimalist software for Linux

  `https://inconsolation.wordpress.com/`

- Awesome Shell: A curated list of awesome command-line apps

  `https://github.com/alebcay/awesome-shell`

- *Pro Git* book by Scott Chacon and Ben Straub and published by Apress available for free

  `https://git-scm.com/book/en/v2`

- Most Useful Command-Line Tools: 50 Cool Tools to Improve Your Workflow, Boost Productivity, and More

  `https://stackify.com/top-command-line-tools/`

Dedicated Pi Projects

Many users use their Raspberry Pi as a sort of dedicated intermediary device between their home network and the "raw" Internet. Some projects that you may be interested in are as follows:

- **Pi-Hole:** A "black hole" for Internet advertisements at `https://pi-hole.net`.

- **Pi-VPN:** A Virtual Private Network server for the Pi at
  `www.pivpn.io`.

- **Firewall and Intrusion Detection:**

  `www.instructables.com/id/Raspberry-Pi-`
  `Firewall-and-Intrusion-Detection-Syst/`.

- **Volumio Audiophile Music Player:** Lets you set up the
  Pi as a dedicated jukebox and music player

  `https://volumio.org/`.

- **OwnCloud:** Create your own cloud server accessible
  from computers, phones, or anywhere. It's like owning
  your own Dropbox

  `https://owncloud.org/`.

- **LAMP Server:** LAMP is short for Linux, Apache, Mysql,
  PHP server. It's essentially an entire web server that's
  ready to use. There's not one massive LAMP installer,
  as it's made up of four very complex parts, but a simple
  online search should deliver several good tutorial sites
  for getting the system set up.

- **RetroPie Arcade:** We discussed RetroPie in the section
  on emulation, but it's a common hobby for creative
  people to design and build physical hardware to go
  with this software. There are everything from handheld
  Game Boy clones up to large wooden arcade-style
  cabinets. I'm not going to recommend any vendors
  here, but a quick Google search for "RetroPie consoles"
  will show you quite a selection.

All of these projects require a Pi dedicated to the task, so you wouldn't want to use your "computer Pi" for these, but they may interest you if you're interested in finding a job for a *second* or *third* Raspberry Pi, which is a lot more common than you might think—new models of the Pi seem to come out awfully fast, leaving many with spare "old" Pi systems to find a use for.

Conclusion

And there you have it.

We've bought, built, and assembled our little Raspberry Pi computer, we've installed the operating system onto the SD card or hard drive, and we set up a user account.

Then we learned the Raspbian desktop interface and installed a bunch of fun and powerful apps.

We then switched over to the command line and installed a selection of even more powerful and customizable tools.

Lastly, we looked at text markup languages and dot-config files, which allow an endless array of customization options.

What have we discovered in all this? That the Raspberry Pi is essentially a regular computer, just smaller, less expensive, and perhaps not quite as expandable as some others. Still, it runs Linux and has all the necessary input and output options, so there is very little that it cannot accomplish. Granted, many of the same apps are slower than those on a new MacBook, but at one-fiftieth of the price, maybe that's a fair trade-off. Only you can say for sure.

Now it's time to get to work!

Index

© Brian Schell 2019
B. Schell, *Computing with the Raspberry Pi*, https://doi.org/10.1007/978-1-4842-5293-2

U

W, X, Y, Z